Keeping Marriages Healthy

David and Teresa Ferguson

INTIMACY PRESS • P.O. Box 201808 • Austin TX 78720-1808
1.800.881.8008 • Fax 512.795.0853 • U.K. 0.800.966.685

ISBN - 0-9642845-8-8

Acknowledgments

"It's not good to be alone" — and God has abundantly blessed us in this writing project, not only with co-laborers from the Intimate Life Ministries team but with many others who support, encourage, and "remove aloneness." Special thanks to:

Alister and Christine Mort, ILM UK Coordinators. Alister and Christine did the significant "shaping" of this resource, adapting and applying content, principles, and practical exercises to the needs of married couples in the UK. We are enormously indebted to the Morts for their gracious, gentle, and hard-working servanthood! Alister is also vicar at St Marks Church, Leamington Spa Warks.

Key UK Ministries and Ministry leaders who have participated in ILM UK "Galatians 6:6" retreats for ministry leaders. Through their participation and subsequent interaction and feedback, these leaders helped confirm the relevance of the principles presented and contributed to the shaping of the content to best serve the UK world:

- Jo and Susie Marriott, pastors of Living Stones Fellowship Eastbourne
- Andy and Dot Croall, Kings Communications
- Lee Rogerson, The Lighthouse Marriage Support Unit

The parishioners of St Marks Church Leamington Spa, especially Sarah and Martyn Jackson, David and Marie Calvert, John and Heather James, Paul and Susan Mileham, Mark Vermes, all of whom contributed significantly to the development of *Keeping Marriages Healthy*, through their helpful support, comments, and suggestions.

Trustees of the ILM Charitable Trust: Simon and Melinda Reading and Martyn Jackson.

Jonathan Mort for his tremendous contribution on graphics and layout and for patiently sharing his computer skills.

Andy Mort for his support when deadlines had to be met by making dinner for the family.

Jenny Mort for her cheerful "I'll get it" whenever the phone rang.

Ike Glass, ILM Executive Team, who spent countless hours under significant time constraints incorporating edits and type-setting this resource.

Andrea Phillips, for the time and effort put into the beautiful design of the cover!

It's a true privilege to offer *Keeping Marriages Healthy* for strengthening marriages in the United Kingdom. Our deepest thanks to all of you who made this resource possible.

May God use this resource to bring about the oneness in marriage He has ordained, for His honor and glory and for our blessing.

David and Teresa Ferguson
August 25, 1998

Contents

Keeping Marriages Healthy

Introduction To Using The Workbook

Welcome to this opportunity to spend time with your marriage partner focusing upon your relationship. It is all too easy because of the many pressures and responsibilities today for such time to be rarely available. We know that the commitment you are now making will benefit you both and that your relationship will deepen and become more satisfying, caring and intimate as a result.

Meeting alongside others

This workbook has been designed to cover eight sessions. It is intended to be used as part of a course alongside others with a leader providing personal insight and example. During each session practical opportunities to experience how greater intimacy can be achieved will be given in the form of short exercises for you to do individually, which will be followed by a time of sharing between the two of you. It must be stressed that whatever is mentioned between you remains personal and private. You will be asked to work on some exercises at home and to begin Marriage Staff Meetings regularly. This is a very important part of the course because it develops a vital pattern that can continue beyond the eight sessions. Although this is fondly termed homework we stress again that you will not be asked to divulge what has been mentioned between you. Should you and your marriage partner need clarification over an issue being covered or support with a particularly sensitive issue for you then the course leaders are available to come alongside.

What will be covered

Fundamental to growing closeness is, a greater understanding of each other's needs followed by a desire to increasingly meet those needs in each other. This is one of the first sessions covered. Recognising that those initial feelings of love that felt so strong and positive can sometimes be pushed aside by more negative emotions will be helpful as we examine the "emotional cup." The power of forgiveness, hindrances to our willingness to forgive and the importance of being able to admit wrong and hurt with confession will be dealt with. Caring, trusting, needing and loving are the four ingredients of a healthy marriage that will be emphasised throughout the workbook but which are also given special attention for one session. Consideration is given to the obstacles we face when truly leaving the childhood home behind, along with our need to be able to mourn and be comforted for childhood hurts. An awareness will be given of the unhealthy patterns we develop in our thinking that can be a barrier to closeness with our marriage partners and cause us unwittingly to "play games" that are unhelpful and even damaging. There are three dimensions to our marriage relationships: spiritual, emotional and physical, and the last session looks at increasing closeness in each area.

Maintaining fitness

Training our bodies in exercise and diet to become physically fit needs to be maintained over time and sustained regularly. Getting fit for one month of the year and then reverting to old habits of no exercise and a poor diet will not produce a physically healthy body. The eleven months of the year will quickly undo all the good achieved in the other one. More effective is a change of lifestyle that can be maintained with a goal that is achievable. In the area of relationships "Keeping Marriages Healthy" gives that sort of opportunity, providing not only the goals but the "how to," to achieve those goals in a way that can go on being practised simply and effectively throughout married life.

God's Plan For Marriage

Remembering the Wedding Day

Whether very recent or many years ago your wedding day marked the start of a new stage in your relationship. Each wedding day is the same in its significance but uniquely different in detail. Those who were married during the war did not have the opportunity for the attention to detail that a 1990's wedding often displays. Weddings in the 1970's were sometimes characterised by informality. A few sandwiches for family and close friends back at the bride's home, a cold salad served buffet style in the church hall or a 5 course dinner at an expensive hotel for several hundred guests; any of these may have been your experience.

Many of you may have had thoughts on the morning of your wedding day, such as "Have we forgotten anything vital? Will the ceremony go well?" Each couple has a unique story of their day. Some experienced amusing incidents.

Other thoughts many people have when they are about to be married concern the magnitude of the step they are about to take. *Am I really ready to be married? Are we sure that we are going to be happy together?* The permanence and the significance of the commitment that will be made during the ceremony means that those vows cannot be taken lightly.

Oneness in Spirit, Soul and Body

To establish a balanced fulfilled marriage God intended us to develop intimacy with our marriage partner in each of these three areas: spirit, soul, and body.

Though we may not have realised it, our wedding vows likely expressed God's plan for intimacy in three dimensions.

Promising to "Love, Honour and Cherish" recognises that our relationship requires emotional intimacy .

"Forsaking all others" refers to the physical dimension to the relationship. "What God has joined together" acknowledges the spiritual dimension in the relationship.

To flourish and survive your marriage needs nourishment and attention in each of these areas. This means that, as the two of you become one, you become best friends growing together in spiritual fellowship and physical closeness.

Relationships in your marriage will grow closer when you share yourselves with one another. (Our society often focuses on one dimension to the complete exclusion of the other two!) The balance and order of priority of these three dimensions will be different before marriage. Some relationships after marriage will get that balance lopsided, expending energies in only one, or at most two, dimensions of the relationship.

The comment "How can we be lovers if we can't be friends?" expresses this.

What about the newly weds who are in love and enjoying their sexual relationship but who still spend a lot of their free time separately with their old friends, or the couple who act more like brother and sister than husband and wife enjoying their friendship but without passion, or the couple so involved in church work that they have no time for fun and recreation? For each of these couples the balance needs to be redressed.

Why God Created Marriage

Why did God creat marriage in the first place? What was His purpose? The first reference to marriage is found in Genesis 2:24 ***"For this reason a man will leave his father and mother and be united to his wife and they shall become one flesh."***
After God created the world, He looked at all that he had made and saw that it was very good. Six times we read in Genesis chapter one that ***"It is Good."*** Adam enjoyed a wonderful creation, an exalted position, he was master of all that he saw, he enjoyed a close relationship with God. Despite all this God observed that it was **not good** that Adam should be **alone** and Eve was created to be his wife in order to remove his aloneness!

God created us with needs that He meets directly and that He desires to meet through intimate human relationships. Why? Because "it is not good for man to be alone." Marriage is on of the divinely provided relationships to remove our aloneness. Family and the church are also His provisions!

Intimacy - - What is it?

What does it take to genuinely remove alonness? Three Old Testament concepts express the essence of what intimacy really is! These three Hebrew words are:

Yada - which means to know deeply. In Psalm 139:1-2, the psalmist praises God for deeply knowing him. Just as God knows us, we need to know each other in marriage in order to experience intimacy.

Sod - which means to disclose or reveal . This is found in Prov. 3:32 "God discloses himself to the upright." Just as we come to know God because He chooses to disclose Himself to us, we must choose to disclose ourselves to each other so that we can deeply know each other.

Sakan - which means "to be of use, service, or profit." Psalm 139:3 speaks of this: "You are intimately acquainted with all my ways!" The psalmist is identifying God's motive for knowing him! He's saying, "God, you know me in order to care about me!" We must also be motivated to know each other in order to care about each other.

Intimacy therefore means to know someone deeply and to be known by them; to be able to disclose innermost thoughts to someone who in turn chooses to reveal themselves to you; lastly it means to be caringly involved with one another, choosing to affirm and build up rather than criticising. We are two complex individuals often with very different personalities, but God provided marriage for us so that we might lovingly know each other deeply in this special intimate way.

God wants us to know Him and enjoy this intimate relationship with Him. He also wants us to deeply know each other in order to be careingly involved with each other in spirit, soul, and body.

Life Events May Challenge Intimacy

Marriages typically pass through predictable "stages" brought on by certain events:

- Early days together.
- Settling into life together.
- First baby, or struggling with infertility.
- Employment /unemployment pressures.
- Growing children.
- Teenage pressures.
- Children leaving home.
- Responsibility for ageing parents.
- Retirement from employment.

During each of these stages relationships will develop and mature as new challenges are faced. Sometimes external pressures or family tensions cause strain on the marriage and previously enjoyed intimacy is lost. The arrival of a baby, the difficulties of making time for one another in the midst of both having demanding and challenging careers, time spent away from home on business trips, teenage years, extended family, ageing parents all create demands on time and emotions. It can become easy for a couple to drift on, reacting to the current most pressing demand upon them, resulting in their own relationship receiving little attention. Too often couples reach the time of "the empty nest" when the children have grown up and left home to find that they have few shared interests. The friendship in their relationship is lacking. In fact the thought of the retirement years and spending even more time together is viewed with dread. Marriages that reach that stage have not collapsed overnight. The eroson has been gradual, often unnoticeable. The "Keeping Marriages Healthy" coarse is designed to equip us to maintain and even deepen our intimacy at every stage, and through every challenge of life. We will learn how to communicate love and affirmation on a regular, daily, basis to deposit strength and build closeness into our marriage relationships.

Finding opportunities to tell each other that you love one another will increase closeness whatever your current stage or situation.

Turn to each other now and say "I am glad that you are my husband/ wife because of your_____________

____

____

____

____

____

____

e.g. sensitivity to others, leadership qualities, willingness to care, wisdom in decision making, loving nature, fun approach, attractive appearance, willingness to stick at something even when it gets difficult.

Increasing Intimacy - Practical Ideas

How might we deepen and develop our spiritual relationship ?

This can be a difficult area for many. It is estimated that only about 1 in 10 couples who are both Christians are praying together. If we are not used to doing so thoughts of praying with each other can make us feel uncomfortable and awkward. Vulnerably praying together can be very precious in your relationship. How do you start? Take time to talk with one another, mentioning matters of personal importance, hold hands and then pray silently. A squeeze of the hand can be the indication that it is over. Verbalising prayer may be more comfortable for others. Remember to concentrate on an item of gratefulness for your marriage partner. Express thankfulness to God for each other.

Read the Bible together or read the same passages during your individual Bible study time.

Intimate Moments has been written to provide daily thoughts on a verse of the Bible that speaks about your relationship with God and with one another.

How can couples who are not both Christians expect to experience spiritual intimacy? By being willing to discuss matters of faith and belief, so being open to consider truths which would take them beyond the emotional and physical. Honestly considering such questions as *Is there a God?, Do I believe in God?, Does Christianity make any sense? Who is Jesus?* will enable a couple to grow in spiritual intimacy.

How might we develop or deepen our friendship?

Time - you can't get close to someone who isn't there. When was your last fun time together without family or friends? What is the next thing you are looking forward to doing together to relax and enjoy being together?

Common Interests - spend time together sharing an interest. Prioritise each other's interests and know what each finds important or enjoyable.

Feelings - when you talk express how you feel. Share anxieties, hurts, joys. This can be a challenge for many but being able to share how you really feel with another will bring closeness. Many extra-marital affairs have begun, not with sexual attraction, but with two people being able to talk about their emotions with one another. Once deep feelings, often hurts and pain, have been shared then the sexual involvement may quickly follow.
Dream together about plans for the future.

Experiencing Romans 12 :15

One way we can deepen freindship oneness is to ***"Rejoice with those who rejoice, .."***

Think about a positive memory, recent or from the past.......a pleasant occasion of when you felt loved, cared for, special.
e.g. a birthday treat, Christmas, receiving a much wanted pet, taking part in a school play, a sporting achievement, an activity shared with a friend, working alongside a parent at something........

Share that positive memory now with your marriage partner.

As your partner shares with you identify what feelings you have for him/her. e.g. happy, glad, joyful, excited.
Express those feelings to your partner "I'm glad that happened; I'm excited for you; that sounds great."
Now swap roles.

What did it feel like to be rejoiced with?

Responding with joy fro something good is an example of being caringly involved with each other. Sharing the good memory is part of vulnerably disclosing ourselves to each other. This exchange is an example of what's involved in knowing each others more deeply.

Later we will experience the second half of that verse as we explore the role comfort has in healing hurt.

How might we deepen our physical relationship?

Sexual intimacy can often be difficult for couples to talk about and can be one of the stress points of a marriage. Talking with one another about dreams, goals, fears, excitements, joys will deepen affection. Feeling that this person is really interested in me, in what I am thinking about and in what I am feeling at the moment will increase sexual intimacy.
Most couples will benefit from increasing the level of non-sexual touching.
The words used when you part and greet one another again can verbalise love and build up affection.

Assess Your Relationship - Where are we?

You are encouraged to assess the level of your intimacy in each of these three dimensions.

- What does it mean to be physically intimate with my marriage partner?
- What does it mean to be a friend to each other?
- What would a spiritual dimension to our relationship involve?

Take a few minutes to reflect on your relationship; and indicate your perception of the degree of intimacy in each dimension. Place a mark on the scale to signify your view of the relationship. Work individually on this. You will be sharing your thoughts later with each other.

The spiritual dimension of our relationship is:

Lacking In Intimacy — Very Intimate

What aspect of your spiritual relationship would you most like to see changed or improved in your marriage?

The emotional or friendship dimension of our relationship is:

Lacking In Intimacy — Very Intimate

What aspect of being a friend to your spouse would you most like to see changed or improved in your marriage?

The physical dimension of our relationship is:

Lacking In Intimacy — Very Intimate

What aspect of your physical closeness would you most like to see changed or improved in your marriage?

Now complete the marital intimacy inventory, each working through it alone. Carefully read each of the fifteen questions and circle the number from 1-5 that is most representative of your response.

Marriage Intimacy Inventory

		Strongly Disagree	Disagree	Neutral	Agree	Strongly Agree
1	My spouse is supportive and encouraging of my personal spiritual growth.	1	2	3	4	5
2	We seem to be good at giving one another undivided attention when listening or talking.	1	2	3	4	5
3	My spouse is attentive and sensitive to my needs in the area of sexual foreplay.	1	2	3	4	5
4	We seem to practise honest confession followed by genuine forgiveness when one of us has hurt the other.	1	2	3	4	5
5	When I'm sharing my feelings, my spouse values them and is sensitive to provide understanding reassurance.	1	2	3	4	5
6	I'm very comfortable communicating to my spouse my sexual desires and preferences.	1	2	3	4	5
7	It would be characteristic for us to share together some of our long range dreams and hopes - even if they seemed silly!	1	2	3	4	5
8	Sharing appreciation and verbalising love are two things my spouse is very good at.	1	2	3	4	5
9	We seem to prioritise frequent times of quality talking and having dates together.	1	2	3	4	5
10	We seem to frequently recount the good times and blessings we have enjoyed as a couple.	1	2	3	4	5
11	I remember special times when my spouse and I shared together in strong emotions, like grief, sadness, joy, or brokenness.	1	2	3	4	5
12	I'm very satisfied with my spouse's sensitivity in meeting my sexual needs.	1	2	3	4	5
13	In many of the important issues concerning values and beliefs, my spouse and I often tend to agree.	1	2	3	4	5
14	Verbalising to my spouse my needs and desires concerning our relationship would be normal for me.	1	2	3	4	5
15	I am satisfied in my spouse's frequency of initiating sexual times together.	1	2	3	4	5

Interpreting Your Score

Add your responses for questions No. 1, 4, 7, 10, 13 and chart your score here:

Spiritual Scale:

0 5 10 15 20 25

Add your responses for questions No. 2, 5, 8, 11, 14 and chart your score here:

Friendship Scale:

0 5 10 15 20 25

Add your responses for questions No. 3, 6, 9, 12, 15 and chart your score here:

Physical Scale:

0 5 10 15 20 25

Did any new insights or questions come to mind as you completed this inventory?

Scatter and share

Using the worksheets : Marriage Intimacy Inventory and Interpreting Your Score, spend time together sharing with each other the results of the inventory and the assessment of intimacy exercise. You are encouraged to think of the good times / blessings in your relationship and begin to verbalise them together.

At the end of this chapter guidelines are provided for you to work on together before the next session, some of which you will have started in the scatter and share time.

Return to group.

Marriage Staff Meetings

Developing and maintaining marriage intimacy will require time - consistently invested in quality sharing. The external stresses of work, managing finances, and bringing up a family need not take their toll on closeness if couples consistently and "together" manage family events before they "manage" you!

How much time - a typical recommendation would be an hour, to an hour and a half, each week set aside for a couple to talk together.

Schedule a time - don't leave it to chance! Lunch on Thursday, Tuesday evening after the children are in bed, Saturday morning breakfast.
If the time has to change each week, arrange the time routinely i.e. Sunday evening.

Prioritise the time - make it "inviolate" as much as possible. The consistency each week is important but the emotional benefit of prioritising one another in this time encourages closeness.

Protect the time - from interruptions and distractions. Find a "quiet" place at home or outside without phones or visitors if possible.

A fearful thought for many couples would be "what in the world would we talk about?"

Staff Meetings - A Typical Agenda

Calendar Co-ordination - for the coming week.
What is planned? What are the children doing and what lifts do they need? Who is working late?
What social activities are planned? (operate from a principle of agreeing on time commitments which affect the family before saying "yes.")
Plan your next time of going out together as a couple and your next family outing.

Discuss Family Goals - monitoring progress and working together.
Written annual goals should be developed for the family and broken down into termly or monthly target dates.
Do the finances look tight this week and how can we all help?
What is our next planned major household expenditure and how could we all better contribute to bring it about?
Have we any new friends that we want to spend time getting to know better this year?
How are our personal goals progressing ....reading, diet, exercise, hobby......and how can we encourage / support one another?

Parenting Plans - it is better to plan and become united than have the children "divide and rule". Discuss significant discipline issues; what seems to be working and what doesn't?

Plan family times together plus individual times for each child. Discuss and agree upon parenting responsibilities for the next week or more......i.e. who is needing help? Who is needing a break?
What goals seem reasonable this term for our children in the areas of behaviour, attitude and responsibilities? How can we work together to achieve them?

Listening Times - one or the other may just need to talk.
Sharing stresses at work or with friendships.
Sharing hopes and dreams.
Sharing feelings and insights about recent moodiness.
Sharing concerns and fears about "us", the children, finances, the future.
You can't argue when one of you is listening.
Give undivided attention, empathy, support and eye contact .

Productive Expression of Needs - lovingly shared hopes for the future. Avoid "you" statements and generalities for example, *"You never spend any time with me!"*
"You always take the children's side against me!"
Use "I" and "me" statements with specifics...............POSITIVELY *"I really miss being alone together and hope we could plan to go out somewhere together soon."*
It would mean a lot to me if we could stay in agreement in front of the children and discuss any differences privately."

Appreciation - for "who" they are and "what" they've done.
Use your weekly "staff" meeting as a reminder that your husband / wife is a blessing to you! They do have good qualities!
Examples: *"Thank you for the extra help you've given this week with the children."*
"The way you greet me when I get in from work means a lot to me."

Homework

During the Keeping Marriages Healthy course the staff meeting will provide opportunity to go over issues covered in the sessions, some of which you may want to develop further once the course is over.

Closing Prayer

Hold hands and using similar words to these together give thanks to God for one another.

You are precious to the Lord Jesus Christ.
You are loved by Him as a special child.
You are precious to me, I am thankful for you.
You are special, I am glad you are my husband/wife.
Let us continue to grow together;
Let us develop our relationship in those three vital areas of emotional, spiritual and physical oneness.
I love you; I thank God for you.

Scatter and Share / Marriage Staff Meeting

1. Begin by telling each other how much you appreciate each other's willingness to work on deepening your marriage intimacy.

2. Discuss the Marriage Intimacy Inventory results.

We suggest that the husband take the initiative and begin sharing his perceptions in each of the areas of intimacy. Share insights or ask questions, in order to both be understood and to understand. The wives would then share in a similar way.

3. Husbands share the specific area in each dimension which they would most like to see change in themselves. Then the wives should share.

Some specific examples of the kinds of things you might express to each other:

"As I look over your responses in the area of spiritual intimacy, I see that I don't encourage you enough spiritually. I'd really like to learn how to change that."

"I see that I'm probably not expressing to you enough just how much I appreciate you and why. I really want to do better at that."

"I can see that I need to give you more of my undivided attention. Would that be helpful to you?"

4. End your staff meeting by holding hands, thanking each other for having the courage to be open and vulnerable in your responses.

What Do We Really Need From Each Other?

Do you remember the Paul Simon song "I am a rock"? Those who live as "a rock" try not to show emotion and protect themselves from experiencing any pain by trying to shut feelings out. For a marriage partner this can produce a lot of hurt.

The following is an example of a couple who are having difficulty experiencing intimacy. As you become briefly familiar with their situation, ask yourself a) What does each person need from the other? b) What would it take to help each person feel more loved in their marriage relationship?

Richard and Jean Jones

Richard often works 50 - 60 hours a week. He earns a good salary but he feels he could still do better. He is self-employed in financial services. Richard and his wife Jean have two children, a 9 year old son and a 6 year old daughter. Whenever he isn't working Richard gives time to his son's football team which he helps coach.

Jean works part-time during school hours temping as a secretary. She also spends a fair amount of time taking both children to various activities and lessons. Secretly Jean wishes that Richard were willing to have another child. She found it very hard when their daughter went to school all day.

Richard is not good at communicating with Jean. By the time he comes home from work or from coaching he just wants to crash out in front of the TV. To Jean he seems distant and unapproachable. She really wants to know what he is thinking and feeling but he never says much. She finds herself lonely much of the time. Talking to her friends just isn't the same. Richard's response to Jean's "Why won't you talk to me ? I'm wondering if you really care about me at all!" is usually "I just don't have that much to say! I spend all day talking to people and I've talked enough."

What do you think Jean needs from Richard? How might Richard help Jean feel more loved or cared for? What do you think Richard needs from Jean? How might Jean help Richard feel more loved or cared for?

It is not good that man should be alone

We have seen from Genesis Chapter 2 that God placed Adam in a perfect environment, with abundant provisions and in a close relationship with Himself. And yet God said ***"It is not good that man should be alone".***

It was "not good" because Adam had been created with needs that God designed to be met in relationships. We need God, *and* we need other people! Needs are a sign of our humanity. Adam had these needs before the Fall. They are not a sign of our sinfulness. God had met Adam's physical and spiritual needs in abundance but his relational needs could be met by another human being. Sometimes God meets those needs directly Himself e.g. when we experience His comfort at a time of bereavement, or His peace in the midst of anxiety. A verse of the Bible can bring encouragement when God speaks through it directly to our situation. Can you think of a time when God met your needs directly?

____
____
____
____
____
____

However, God also chooses to involve other people to meet our relational needs and for this reason God established marriage, the family and the church. Within these relationships God wants us ***to love as we have been loved*** (John 4:11); ***to comfort as we have been comforted*** (2 Cor 1:4) *and* ***to forgive as we have been forgiven*** (Ephes 4:32). We receive first from God and with grateful hearts we share with others. To experience intimacy within marriage, the family and the church there needs to be mutual giving and receiving.

Can you think of a time when God involved others to meet your needs?

____
____
____
____
____
____

For those who are married God intends that our marriage be the primary relationship through which there is giving and receiving to meet needs.

Needs Met and Unmet

Amongst our several physical needs are those for food and sleep. Depending upon how much sleep we have had we either feel rested or irritable. If we have sufficient food we feel satisfied, if insufficient we become weak.
If our basic relational needs are met there is fulfilment, we feel loved and close. If needs are unmet there is frustration and we feel irritated, angry and hurt.

If one partner in the marriage hasn't received any attention, affection or appreciation they can become vulnerable to moodiness, rejection, retaliation, become uncommunicative and turn inward. It is also possible for that person to look elsewhere for those emotional needs to be met.

A need cannot be met if the other partner is totally unaware of it. This may arise from a lack of observation or not knowing the partner well enough, or from that partner being totally unwilling or unable to communicate what the need is, taking the "There's nothing wrong" approach even when gently asked. Unmet need is never easy to live with.

Phil 4:19 says ***"And my God will meet all your needs according to His glorious riches in Christ Jesus".***
This verse makes no sense at all unless we accept that needs are God given, an integral part of our being and as God intended us to be.
God involves others in our lives,

giving us relationships in which we can give to each other. As we freely receive from God so we freely give to each other.

We will never grow out of our neediness. Just as a child thrives when receiving affection, attention, and affirmation, so our lives are more fulfilled when we go on receiving these things.

See the chart "Understanding Intimacy Needs" for more insights concerning the "Potential and Pain of Intimacy Needs," page 25.

God says to us

It is OK to have needs and God asks us to deal with them together. In Rev 3:17 we read that the church in Laodicea which said of itself ***"I do not need a thing"*** was told ***"you do not realise that you are wretched, pitiful, poor, blind and naked"***. Rather we need to be willing to vulnerably admit our needs and to minister to one another remembering that Jesus modelled this. In Matthew 26:38 we read ***"My soul is overwhelmed with sorrow to the point of death. Stay here and keep watch with me"*** Jesus was in need, he shared with his friends that he longed that they should be alongside him. Instead of a self-sufficient attitude he showed his friends that he was "poor in spirit".

10 Commonly Identified Intimacy Needs

Acceptance - Looking beyond faults, differences, irritations to see your partner's worth. An unconditional commitment to an imperfect person.

Appreciation - Recognising the special things about your partner and thanking him/her for being who they are.

Affection - Greeting with a kiss. Verbalising "I care for you", "I'm here for you." Hugging and touching non-sexual and sexual. "I love you."

Approval - Noticing the things that a partner does and being grateful or complimentary. Not taking things for granted. Looking for the best rather than always pointing out the flaws.

Attention - Being together, doing things together. Taking time to listen, remembering to tell each other about the day. Showing interest without criticism.

Comfort - Sensitively showing concern at a partner's disappointment or hurt. Taking seriously another's feelings. Hurting with and for another's pain.

Encouragement - Helping a partner to keep going when enthusiasm has gone. Showing interest in their concerns. Not rushing in to take over a task from a struggling partner when encouragement would result in the task being completed.

Respect - Honouring each other. Never putting each other down in front of others. Using humour sensitively; being willing to be serious when a joke would be hurtful and imply criticism.

Security - Knowing that security is found in strong, reliable relationships rather than material goods and making a priority of reminding a partner of your long term commitment to them. Doing the "little things" with consistency.

Support - Giving the message to a partner that you can be counted on when needed. Noticing times of particular stress and offering help. Sharing tasks.

Top 10 Intimacy Needs

We all need the above in some measure and especially at particular times. However there will be certain of these relational needs that you will enjoy receiving over and above the others. You are invited to choose which are your top three needs and guess which 3 needs your marriage partner most enjoys receiving.

Intimacy Needs

Myself		Partner
☐	**Acceptance** - deliberate and ready reception with a favourable positive response (Rom. 15:7)	☐
☐	**Affection** - to communicate care and closeness through physical touch (Rom. 16:16)	☐
☐	**Appreciation** - to communicate with words and feelings a personal gratefulness for another (1Cor.11:2)	☐
☐	**Approval** - expressed commendation; to think and speak well of (Rom. 14:18)	☐
☐	**Attention** - to take thought of another and convey appropriate interest and support; to enter into another's "worlds" (1 Cor. 12:25)	☐
☐	**Comfort** - (empathy) - to come alongside with word, feeling and touch; to give consolidation with tenderness (Rom. 12:15)	☐
☐	**Encouragement** - to urge forward and positively persuade toward a goal (1 Thes.5:11, Heb.10:24)	☐
☐	**Respect** - to value and regard highly; to convey great worth (Rom. 12:10)	☐
☐	**Security** - confidence of harmony in relationships; free from threat of harm (Rom.12:16a)	☐
☐	**Support** - come alongside and gently help carry a load (Gal. 6:2)	☐

Now compare lists and make a note of the three needs you have chosen alongside those your partner has chosen for themselves.

Your Needs	Partner's Needs
1. ______________________	1. ______________________
2. ______________________	2. ______________________
3. ______________________	3. ______________________

As you compare lists notice how many of your needs are the same.

0 the same ☐

1 the same ☐

2 the same ☐

3 the same ☐

What happens if the two lists have only one or even none the same? First of all be reassured that this is quite likely to be the case. We are more likely to be married to someone whose top needs are different from our own. What can happen however is a tendency to give to our partner the things we would actually like to receive ourselves. One partner has a top need for affection and can't quite understand why the other seems ungrateful at all the affection being offered to them, when in fact respect would be more appreciated.

What about those whose two lists are very similar? This combination may result in needs being satisfied although there can be a danger that needing something yourself doesn't mean you know how to give it to others. Hearing from each other insight into how a need can best be met will be helpful.
For example *"I really enjoy being greeted at the door when I come in from work. This shows me your affection."* Or
"Going for a short walk together in the evening when we can talk about our day means a lot to me. I really feel attention from you in that way."

An additional exercise is available on identifying the top needs. This will help you explore further which are the needs you feel strongest. Knowing your partner's greatest needs will enable you to talk about how best you can meet them for him/her. This exercise can be done at home and discussed during this week's staff meeting.

Intimacy Needs Assessment Tool

Instructions

Please answer these questions by placing the appropriate number beside each sentence

Strongly Disagree	Disagree	Neutral	Agree	Strongly Agree
-2	-1	0	+1	+2

.... 1. It's important that people receive me for who I am - even if I'm a little "different".

.... 2. It's very important to me that my financial world is in order.

.... 3. I sometimes become "weary in well doing".

.... 4. It's vital to me that others ask my opinion.

.... 5. It's important to me that I receive physical hugs, warm embraces etc.

.... 6. I feel good when someone "enters my world."

.... 7. It's important to me to know "where I stand" with those who are in authority over me.

.... 8. It is particularly meaningful when someone notices that I need help and then offers to get involved.

.... 9. When I feel overwhelmed, I want someone to come alongside me and help.

.........10. I feel blessed when someone recognises and shows concern for how I am feeling emotionally.

.........11. I always like to know that what I "do" is of value and meaningful to others.

.........12. Generally speaking, I do not like a lot of solitude.

.........13. It means a lot to me for loved ones to be the first to say "I love you."

.........14. I resist being seen only as part of a large group - my individuality is important.

.........15. I am particularly blessed when a friend calls to listen and encourage me.

.........16. It's important to me that people acknowledge me not just for what I do but for who I am.

.........17. I feel best when my world is orderly and somewhat predictable.

.........18. When I have worked hard on a project, I am pleased for people to acknowledge my work and express gratitude.

.........19. I am unhappy at work unless I am surrounded by some co-workers who enjoy my company.

.........20. It's particularly encouraging to me when I realise that others notice my good points.

.........21. I sometimes feel discouraged.

.........22. I want to be treated with kindness and equality by all, regardless of my race, gender, looks or status.

.........23. The physical aspect of marriage is / would be very important to me.

.........24. I love it when someone wants to spend time with me.

.........25. I am particularly pleased when my boss says "Well done."

.........26. It is very important to me for someone to hold me and hug me after I have a bad day.

.........27. Though I feel confident about what I "do" (my talents, gifts etc.), I always sense that I need other people's input and help.

.........28. Written notes and calls expressing sympathy after the death of a loved one, health problem or other stressful events are very meaningful to me.

.........29. I feel good when my spouse shows satisfaction with who I am.

.........30. I enjoy being spoken of or mentioned in front of a group of people.

.........31. I would be described as a "touchy / feely" person.

.........32. When a decision is going to affect my life, it's important to me that I have a "say" in the decision.

.........33. I am particularly blessed when someone shows interest in current projects that I am working on.

.........34. I appreciate trophies, plaques and special gifts which are a permanent reminder of something significant that I have done.

.........35. I sometimes worry about the future.

.........36. When I'm introduced to a new environment, I immediately search for a new group of people to make contact with.

.........37. The thought of change (moving, a new job etc.) produces anxiety for me.

.........38. It bothers me when people are prejudiced against someone just because they dress or act differently.

.........39. It's necessary for me to be surrounded by friends and loved ones who will be there "through thick and thin."

.........40. I am particularly pleased by written notes and expressions of gratitude.

.........41. To know that someone is constantly praying for me is very meaningful.

.........42. I am particularly bothered by people who want to control.

.........43. I feel particularly good when I receive unmerited and spontaneous expressions of love.

.........44. I am pleased when someone looks me in the eye and really listens to me talk.

.........45. I am particularly pleased when people commend me for a godly characteristic that I exhibit.

.........46. I never want to be alone when experiencing hurt or trouble; it's important to me to have a close friend who will be with me.

.........47. I really don't enjoy working on a project by myself, I prefer to have a "help-mate" on every project.

.........48. It's important to me to feel a "part of the group".

.........49. I really respond to someone who tries to understand me emotionally and who shows me loving concern.

.........50. When working on a project, I would rather work with a team of people than by myself.

INTERPRETATION OF QUESTIONS

1. Add up your responses (-2,-1,0,+1,+2) to questions

1----------
38--------
48--------
36--------
19--------
Total----------

These responses relate to the need for
ACCEPTANCE

2. Add up your responses to questions

2-----------
37----------
39----------
17----------
35----------
Total-----------

These responses relate to the need for
SECURITY.

3. Add up your responses to questions

40-----------
18-----------
20-----------
34-----------
16-----------
Total------------

These responses relate to the need for
APPRECIATION

4. Add up your responses to questions

3 -----------
33----------
21----------
15----------
41----------
Total----------

These responses relate to the need for
ENCOURAGEMENT

5. Add up your responses to questions

4--------------
22------------
42------------
14------------
32------------
Total -------------

These responses relate to the need for
RESPECT

6. Add up your responses to questions

5-----------
31---------
13----------
43---------
23---------
Total----------

These responses relate to the need for
AFFECTION

7. Add up your responses to questions

6-----------
24---------
30---------
12---------
44---------
Total---------

These responses relate to the need for
ATTENTION

8. Add up your responses to questions

7-----------
25----------
11----------
45----------
29----------
Total----------

These responses relate to the need for
APPROVAL

9. Add up your responses to questions

49----------
26----------
10----------
46----------
28----------
Total-----------

These responses relate to the need for
COMFORT

10 Add up your responses to questions

9------------
47-----------
27-----------
8------------
50-----------
Total------------

These responses relate to the need for
SUPPORT

1. What were your three highest totals? Which needs do they represent?

2. What were your three lowest totals? Which needs do they represent?

3. Which were your spouse's highest and lowest totals?

Meeting Needs

Giving to each other in ways that makes each feel loved and cared for will be very significant in building happiness and fulfilment in marriage.

Turn to one another and say, "I really feel loved by you when

____

____

____

____

____

____

e.g. "you phone me to tell me what time you will be home", " you ask me first before making any arrangements to play sport with your friends", " you value my opinion when choosing new clothes", " you bring me a cup of tea in bed", " you kiss me goodbye in the morning", "you take time to listen to me when I'm down".

This is not an opportunity to say " I wish you would........", rather one to encourage your marriage partner in something they are already doing.

You may like to make a note of the ways in which your marriage partner has expressed feeling loved and cared for by you.

____

____

____

____

____

____

Another exercise, Special to Receive can help in discovering what each other really finds special. Mark those items listed next that really appeal to you. During the Scatter and Share time find out from your partner what he/she would most like to receive, and mark those down. Take opportunity in the next few weeks to give to each other from this list. The items chosen will also give insight into your partner's top needs. A list like this is very limited so you might like to take time to talk about what you would like added.

Special to Recieve

Choose four items and mark them in the Myself column

Partner	Myself	
☐	☐	Holding hands
☐	☐	Going for a walk
☐	☐	An unexpected hug
☐	☐	Finding a love note
☐	☐	Receiving a surprise gift
☐	☐	Being served a favourite meal
☐	☐	Being told "I love you"
☐	☐	Helping with the children
☐	☐	Being approached sexually
☐	☐	Seeing the house tidy
☐	☐	Having the lawn mown
☐	☐	Receiving compliments on looks
☐	☐	Taking a shower together
☐	☐	A surprise night out
☐	☐	Getting a back massage
☐	☐	Having dinner together
☐	☐	Being praised for achievements
☐	☐	Having a quiet conversation

Any additional items

Understanding Intimacy Needs

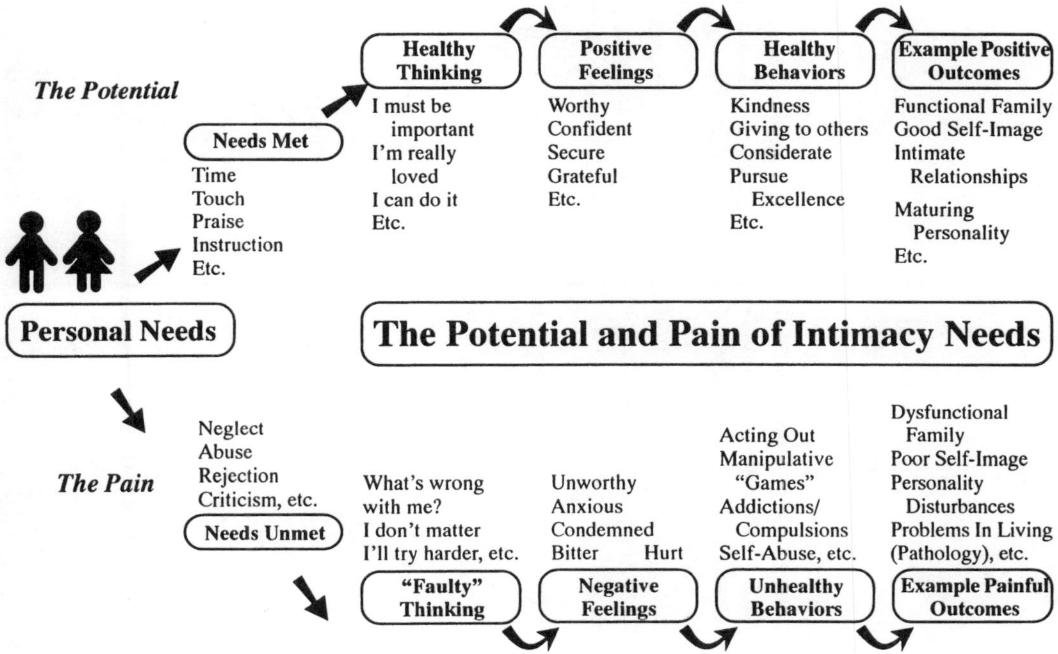

The result of unmet need?

There are three main dangers for us when needs are unmet .

1. **Selfishness** - we can look to take from others instead of giving. Within a marriage each partner can become preoccupied with their own needs, looking always to take what they consider to be their right to have, never focusing on giving first to the other. Taking for ourselves is never satisfying, and such a relationship will soon crumble.
2. **Self-reliance** - believing that all that is needed to survive and be happy can be found within oneself. Families can encourage self reliance and discourage showing true feelings to others. The ability to stuff feelings down inside is then regarded as a virtue. Those who have experienced a lot of hurt or pain in childhood may have wrongly learnt that to survive they mustn't let anyone see their hurt. "Big boys don't cry". Sadly it is difficult also to feel positive emotions, to feel loved by another, if the important thing has been to be totally self-sufficient.
3. **Self-condemning** - believing that they are not really loveable, unworthy, feeling that they are responsible for everything, particularly the things that go wrong. Such a person feels guilty that they have needs and finds it very difficult to receive.

Scatter and Share

Share with each other about the needs and reflections you have about this session. Talk about the items you have ticked giving ideas about what would make you feel loved and cared for. Make a note of the things your partner would enjoy.

Return to the group

This has been an important opportunity to find out about what your marriage partner really needs. You may have gained personal insight into your own needs and understood why your behaviour or deeds have been as they have. Understanding the need beneath the deed and committing to meet that need in each other will increase marital intimacy.

Closing Prayer

Hold hands and thank God that He has given you each other. Ask Him to increase your understanding of each other's needs. Commit to one another before Him your willingness to make meeting your partner's needs a priority.

Scatter and Share / Marriage Staff Meeting

Set aside at least one hour sometime before the next session. In addition to any planning, calendar co-ordination, etc., (See "Marriage Staff Meeting" handout from Session 1):

1) Spend a few minutes talking about the Top Ten Intimacy Needs exercise. Consider asking each other specifically how you might meet one or more of each other's three priority needs this week. If there is anything you don't understand, inquire further. For example, "I'd like to meet your need for encouragement, but I'm not sure exactly how I could go about it . Would you be willing to tell me more how I could encourage you right now?"

2) If you have not already completed the "Special to Receive" exercise. Do so, then:

a) Share your responses.

b) How accurate were you in predicting your partner's responses? If your partner's responses surprised you, take some time to reflect and discuss possible reasons for this.

c) See if you can identify needs from the "Top Ten" list which would be met through the particular "choice". For example, "Holding hands" would probably meet our need for affection, or possibly security. See if there is also a correlation between the choices you selected for yourself and the three needs which you selected as your priority in the previous exercise.

d) Make a note of your partner's responses on your sheet. Commit to initiating at least one "choice" which your spouse selected sometime this week!

3) Share any insights you may have concerning the hindrances to intimacy — Selfishness, Self-reliance, Self Condemnation,

4) Close your staff meeting by holding hands and praying specifically for yourself that God would continue to help you become the husband or wife that He wants you to be.

What Is Filling Your Emotional Cup?

When our God-given relational needs are met, we experience intimacy; when our needs are unmet, we experience hurt and loss. We might express this truth as an "intimacy equation":

Intimacy Needs + Met = Feeling special, loved, cared for.

But there is another all-important "intimacy equation":

Intimacy Needs - Unmet = Feeling unimportant, unloved, uncared for, hurt.

We have seen that we feel loved and cared for when our needs are met, but unmet need produces hurt. Within any marriage we are going to experience misunderstandings, disappointments, let-downs, hurts, rejections. Many times these will be unintentional but they will still cause us pain. No one can meet their marriage partner's needs perfectly. Hurt is inevitable. The question then is "What are we doing with the hurt we are experiencing?"

Consider these three scenarios.

Scenario One

It was an ordinary Monday evening. John sat in the living room watching TV. Helen was in the kitchen tidying up after their meal. The phone rang and John answered it. Helen could tell from his conversation that it must be Kevin, an old school friend of John's.

"That sounds great that you will be in the area next weekend. Of course you can come and stay with us. Helen won't mind. No I'm sure she won't mind. We don't have any plans that can't be changed and its ages since I saw you. Tell you what, I'll get us some tickets for the match on Saturday. It will be just like old times."

Helen finished drying up. Her eyes focused on the envelope pinned to the notice board. The envelope contained theatre tickets for next Saturday. John had known how hard it had been to get them and he had promised to take her. It was to have been a romantic weekend just for the two of them. Instead of that she knew John was likely to suggest she ask someone else to go with her, leaving him free to follow up the match with a visit to the pub, just like old times.

What is Helen feeling at the moment?

____

____

What does she need and why?

____

____

Scenario Two

James had left work early and had made special arrangements including booking a hotel. He wanted this weekend to be absolutely memorable for his wife and himself.
It was their tenth anniversary. James and Paula's getaway weekend was getting off to a rough start, however. The weather forecaster's "partly cloudy" had turned into torrential rain. As they left the motorway it was getting difficult to see the road signs.

James glanced over to Paula "Would you mind getting the map out ready love, just in case we need it?"
Paula's irritation was thinly disguised as she reached towards the glove compartment. "I thought you would have planned the route before we set off. I can't see the map in this light. We are miles from anywhere. If we get lost there will be no one to ask. You've always had a lousy sense of direction. What if the car breaks down? When we do get there, we are not going to be able to go out in all this rain and I bet this hotel is miles from anywhere and there'll be absolutely nothing to do in wet weather. Oh James I just know our weekend is going to be miserable".

What do you think James is feeling at the moment?

____

____

What is he needing and why?

____

____

Scenario Three

During the wedding preparation session with their minister Tracy and Brian were asked to give some information about their family background. Brian was asked to go first.

"I had a really good childhood and my Dad especially had a lot of time for me. We used to go fishing and we went away camping together in the summer. I hope someday that I can be that kind of father to my-----"
Suddenly they heard an audible sigh from Tracy. She reached for a tissue and blew her nose. The minister turned to her and said "Tracy would you like to tell us how your father showed his affection and appreciation?"

Tracey fought back the tears, but managed to reply, "My Dad never gave me any attention . He was always too busy. I still don't know if he loves me or not. My Mum says he does, but I've never felt it. It hurts so much because my Dad is the most important man in my life - and he always will be!"

What do you think is going on in Brian as he hears Tracy's remarks about her father?

____

____

What is he feeling?

____

____

What does he need at the moment?

____

____

What are Tracy's emotions?

____

____

What is she needing at this moment?

____

____

When we experience physical pain, for instance picking up a pan that burns us, we immediately do something to stop that pain continuing; we put the pan down!

How do we deal with emotional pain?

In our brain is an area which can be compared to a small cup which deals with our emotions and feelings. If our "emotional cup" is filled with positive emotions because our needs are met, then our cup will overflow with love, joy and peace. However, negative feelings filling our cup can crowd out positive emotions. We are left experiencing such things as hurt bitterness, anger, guilt, fear, anxiety and stress.

Hurt

The intial emotional response to unmet needs is hurt, sadness, disappointment. We may not consciously feel the pain, but it is there.

Anger

When we are hurt our pain is often masked by anger. Our hurt feelings leave us saddened and vulnerable to more pain and so in order to defend ourselves we turn outward and become angry at others.

Mark 3:5 tells us that ***"Jesus looked round at them in anger and was deeply distressed at their stubborn hearts...."*** He knew that the Pharisees were plotting his death and that they had no compassion for the man with disabilities that He was going to heal. Jesus shows here how anger is a reaction to hurt.

Recognising that underneath anger is hurt gives us understanding that if we show care for the hurt then the anger will be softened. Prov 15:1 ***"A gentle answer turns away wrath, but a hard word stirs up anger".***

Anger can be expressed in different ways. It can be impatience, a quick temper, depression, jealousy, suspicion, sarcasm or stony silence.

Fear

Our unmet need can produce not only hurt and anger but also fear. If we are hurt we not only feel that pain but we also fear more hurt in the future. If something we have done is criticised and ridiculed we feel the pain deeply now but we also fear future failures as well.

Fear can also take several forms. Withdrawal may result, avoiding situations that might bring further hurt. Thinking that being in charge will minimise future pain, another response can be to become controlling. Fear can result in perfectionism, believing that a perfect performance will reduce the chance of hurt. Trying to numb out fear and anxiety can lead others to addiction of alcohol or drugs.

Guilt and Shame

Hurt and anger can lead to guilt. Retaliation for hurt received may mean we hurt others. We can attack and then feel guilt for the hurt we have caused.
Shame and condemnation may also be felt but this isn't related to specific acts and therefore can't be confessed and forgiven in the way guilt is dealt with. Condemnation makes us feel everything is our fault. It attacks our self-esteem and makes us feel a failure and responsible for the hurt we have received.

Emotional Capacity

Symptoms of a 'Full Cup'

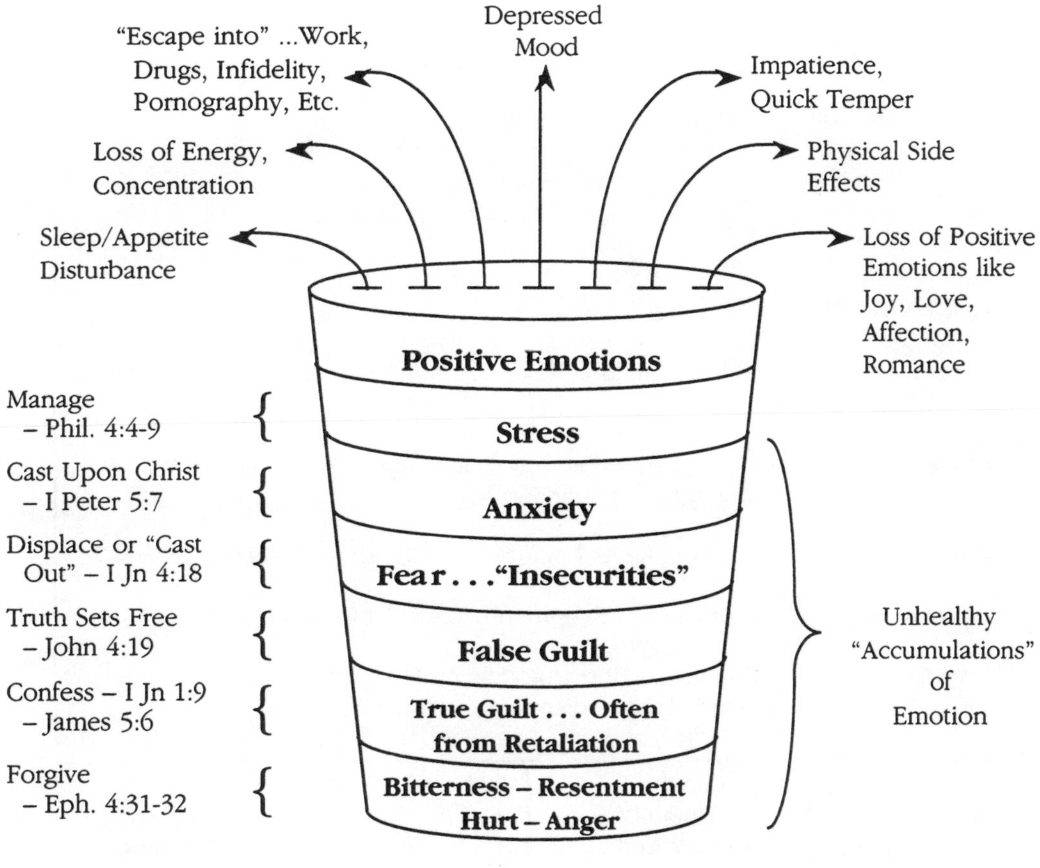

Problems with which we struggle.

What is filling your emotional cup?
Does your behaviour show that your cup is filling with negative emotions?

Sleep problems -	feeling tired all the time unable to sleep
Powerful moods -	irrational fears depression anxiety, worrying unnecessarily
Lack of temper control -	impatient easily angered
Problems associated with eating -	over eating/not eating comfort eating
Loss of energy -	inability to concentrate inability to feel motivated
Loss of positive emotions -	no fun any more apparent coldness unromantic unable to give or receive love
Other "symptoms"	______________________________

Emptying the cup

We can only hold so much emotion. If our cup is full, where have the unhealthy emotions come from?

Hurts	How and by whom have I felt "wounded" by words or by actions?
Anger	Whom do I avoid, reject, criticise, ignore, retaliate against?
Bitterness	Whom do I wish harm on, talk evil of, strive not to be like?
True Guilt	What have I done that has hurt, rejected, wronged, wounded, been disrespectful towards?

The first step in emptying the negative emotions building in our cup is to identify our specific hurts. Many of us carry round a lot of marital hurts that we have never tried to identify. We just know we hurt but we don't know what to do about it.

Hurts also come from outside the marital relationship and contribute to the overflowing of our cup in unhealthy symptoms. This session deals with healing marital hurt. Comforting our marriage partners for hurts received from others will be addressed later.

Healthy marriages heal and resolve inevitable hurts rather than ignoring them or retaliating.
Where there is hurt, anger, or fear, there is a need to minister to it.

How to minister healing for the hurts I have caused my marriage partner.

The first step in breaking the pain cycle is to identify the hurt. Once that has been done confess the hurt to God and then to your marriage partner. Admit it was wrong. Don't rationalise or blame anyone else.

Don't analyse the situation and explain away your responsibility . Try to understand the hurt from your partner's point of view. Your partner may be hurting about something that makes no sense to you. If the hurt is felt it needs caring for.
Complete the following exercise working separately.

Identifying the hurt - Healing Emotional Hurts 1

"Put away all bitterness and anger – and be kind, tender hearted, forgiving each other ……" Ephesians 4 : 31-32

1a. ALONE list ways in which I have hurt my spouse and our marriage.

(it may be preferable to write on a separate piece of paper rather than in this workbook at this point)

Examples: selfish, critical/negative, sensitive, disrespectful, verbally abusive, unsupportive, ungrateful, wrong priorities, rejecting, unforgiving, (specific hurtful events, fights, arguments or "scenes" may need confession – use extra paper as needed!)

1b. Confess to God and receive His forgiveness.

I John 1:9 "If we confess He (God) is faithful and just to forgive us and to cleanse us from all unrighteousness"
Example : God I have deeply hurt you and _______(my spouse) by my____
These are very wrong and I ask you to forgive me. Thank you for your forgiveness and I ask you to change me into the kind of person I need to be.

Don't list hurts about which your partner is not aware.
Use your knowledge about his/her needs to identify ways that hurt will have been felt.

It is important that you first consider ways in which you have hurt your partner. However in order to identify the hurts in your cup so that healing can take place you may also list ways you have been hurt. You will need to work individually first.

Identifying the hurt - Healing Emotional Hurts 2

"Put away all bitterness and anger – be kind, tender hearted forgiving each other…" Ephesians 4:31-32

You are asked to list ways in which you have been hurt by your spouse. This is not a time to get angry or to blame. There is no need to bring up past hurts about which confession and forgiveness have taken place already and from which you no longer feel pain. List the hurts using feeling statements.
e.g. *"I felt hurt and rejected when you pulled away from me the other night in bed"*
"I felt unappreciated when you didn't notice I had prepared your favourite meal."
"I missed your attention when you kept looking at the TV when I was telling you about my difficult day".

ALONE list ways in which I have been hurt by my spouse and our marriage.
(it may be preferable to write on a separate piece of paper rather than in this workbook at this point)

Examples: selfish, critical/negative, insensitive, disrespectful, verbally abusive, unsupportive, ungrateful, unfaithful, wrong priorities, rejecting, unforgiving (specific hurtful events fights, arguments or "scenes" may need confession - use extra paper as needed).

Scatter and Share

Using the empty cup draw a line to represent how full of negative emotions you currently feel your emotional cup to be. Share with each other which feelings you are most aware of both negative and positive. Respond to each other with caring words and concern.

Return to the group

Identifying the hurt is the first part of the process to empty the emotional cup of marital hurt. Next session looks further at confession and forgiveness. Use the time before the next session to increase your understanding of your partner's hurts.

Homework

Spend some time quietly before God with your list reflecting on the ways you have hurt your partner.

Prayer

Holding hands, thank God for your experience of His forgiveness and healing. Commit yourselves to Him and pray for openness and receptivity of His healing in your marriage.

Scatter and Share /Marriage Staff Meeting

In addition to any calendar co-ordination, planning, goal evaluation you need to do, using the Emotional Capacity diagram as a reference,

1. Express to your spouse that you sincerely desire to heal the hurts of your marriage.

2. Share with each other the symptoms of "emotional cup overflow" that each of you identified. Which of these would you most like to see changed in yourself?
(For instance, I have a hard time sleeping, I'm irritable, quick-tempered.)

3. Share with each other: What emotions do you find within yourself which may relate to other relationships? (For example, I only seem to hear from my brother when he needs something. I'm angry at my boss for not giving me the rise I deserved.)

4. Pray for one another as you seek to help empty hurts from your partner's 'cup'.

[If you haven't already, do everything you can to set aside an hour or so to make the two lists of emotional hurts. Pray, asking God to show you the truth about what should be identified on both lists. In our next session, we will learn specifically how to deal with both of these lists.]

Healing Hurts Through Confession, Forgiveness and Comfort

Let's consider again our "emotional cups" and the feelings which may have accumulated, especially hurt. Some of the pain has come from our marriages. And some of the pain was already there prior to, or apart from our marriage relationships. In this session we begin by addressing how to care for the hurt and sadness from sources other than our marriages. Then we will address how our marriage hurts can be healed.

Mourning and comforting

Listen to what is happening between Susan and John in this sketch. It may be helpful to run through it twice, concentrating first on the emotion arising between Susan and her mother and deciding what effect John's response is likely to have on his wife. Secondly decide on the category each of John's responses falls into. Finally reflect upon what makes John's comforting words effective.

The Categories of response

Logic and Reasoning
Pep Talk
Anger
Being the Martyr
Advice/Instruction
Minimising
Personal Fear/Anxiety

Setting

John and Susan have been married for ten years. Susan is about to have an upsetting encounter with her mother who is in a nursing home. When Susan returns home, she shares with John the incident with her mother. The proper response is for John to comfort her, but instead, John gives various unproductive responses. Finally, he speaks words of genuine comfort.

[Susan and her mother are at the nursing home]

Susan: Mother, you've got to eat! You can't go on starving yourself to death.
Mother: I'm not hungry.
Susan: Mum, don't be difficult, Not only are you not eating, but the nursing staff say you've been staying in your room all by yourself. You need to get out and make some friends.
Mother: That nursing staff have no business watching me like a hawk.
Susan: They're not watching you like a hawk. They care for you and want you safe and healthy.
Mother: They don't care about me and neither do you!
Susan: Mother! How can you say that?
Mother: It's true.
Susan: It is not! I come to see you at

least every other day.
Mother: Why not every day?
Susan: Mother, I've got three small children to take care of; sometimes I just can't get away
Mother: Like I said, you just don't care.
Susan: Mother....!
Mother: You go now.... come back when you can

[Later in the day Susan is at home with her husband]

Susan: John, I'm so upset. I went to see my mother today. She is refusing to eat her meals, she's been driving the nursing staff crazy, and when I was about to leave, she accused me of not caring for her.
John: Susan, I've told you before, old people are like that, if you were to take a poll of everyone who has a parent in that nursing home they'd have similar frustrations. You need to face the facts, dear, it's just part of the circle of life; parents get old and they need to be taken care of.

Type of response?
(see list on page 36 - pick from logic & reasoning, pep talk, anger, etc.)

John: Do you remember we went through the same ordeal with my parents. I can remember being so frustrated with my dad that I thought I was going to have to hire a full-time nurse. And my dad wouldn't even go into a nursing home, he insisted on staying in his house. At least at the nursing home they cook meals for your mother, and they're available in case of emergency. All in all this has come at a bad time for me; I'm really busy at the office and I don't need the extra burden of having to deal with your mum.

Type of response ?

John: That's terrible, but the world doesn't revolve around your mum. Let's not make a big deal about this; it's not the only thing in our lives. There's plenty of good things to concentrate on - Tim's football match is this afternoon, we're going off together next weekend. Don't let this one event get you down. What did you say was for dinner?

Type of response?

John: Oh great! Susan, that's ridiculous. You've been a wonderful daughter to your Mum. No one would ever accuse you of being unloving and uncaring. You're one of the most caring people I know. Don't let it get you down! We've been through tough times before and you've handled them OK! I've no doubt that you'll do it again!

Type of response?

John: Well, it's time we do something about it. Lets call the nursing home administrator and get her input, I'm sure it's not the first time something like this has happened. We might need to make a fuss. Remember the squeaky wheel gets the oil and if you want them taking care of her, you're going to have to make some noise. As for the meals, believe me, your mother will eat if she gets hungry enough. Perhaps a change in diet would be good.

Type of response?

John: That's bad news. We're already paying through the nose for nursing home care. If your mother gets to the point of needing a personal nurse the cost will sky-rocket. How in the world can we do that and help Jill go to university? And with all the pressure I'm under at work, I don't need another problem.

Type of response?

John : That makes me so mad! Your mother can control what she does. She's just doing it to get attention. She needs to realise that she's hurting you by her ridiculous statements. I'm tempted to call her and give her a piece of my mind. And as for the nursing home's administration - I'll have social services down on them so fast, their heads will spin!

Type of response?

John: Susan, I'm really sorry that you had a hurtful encounter with your Mum. (John reaches out and hold's Susan's hand.) It hurts me to see you hurt. I know you love your Mum, and it's hard to hear her say things like that. Next time you go to the nursing home, let me go with you, just to give you support.

Type of response?

Whilst the words of comfort are the most effective in showing John's care for his wife, they may sound rather different to the words we have grown used to using. Comforting words often don't come to our minds as quickly as the logical explanation, the pep talk or the "It's not really as bad as you think" response. In comforting we are using words that speak of our emotional involvement with the painful situation being described. It means we have left our concerns behind for a moment to concentrate on our partner's hurt, we leave our own "world" behind to enter theirs with them.

Comforting your Spouse

Comfort for a childhood memory

Romans 12 :15 "..................and mourn with those who mourn"
Think about a painful memory from your childhood before the age of 12......a memory of a time you felt lonely, unloved, misunderstood, rejected, afraid, un-cared for.

e.g. an embarrassing moment, a time when failure was experienced such as not getting a part in a school play or sport team, a family tragedy experienced, being called names, witnessing something frightening........................

Share this unpleasant memory and your painful feelings about it with your marriage partner.

What feelings do you have for your partner as you hear this painful memory expressed to you? (You may find yourself feeling anger towards the person who caused this hurt. Concentrate instead on your feelings for your husband/wife having to experience this pain.)

Express your feelings of sadness and sorrow now in comforting words such as *"It saddens me that.......I hurt for you that you..........because I care, I love you. You must have felt so alone. That must have been so painful."*

Now swap roles

Perhaps you heard something you have never heard before. You may have been familiar with the event but heard it in a different way.

Recalling the memory and being comforted did nothing to change the circumstances but it will give the opportunity to remove your aloneness in the pain. What did it feel like to have your partner feel "with you" and "for you" in your pain?

Confession, forgiveness, and comfort of marriage hurt.

In every marriage, conflict, difficulty, and pain is inevitable. In even the best of marriages, both husbands and wives make mistakes, forget things, overlook needs, get too busy, or even take each other for granted. There really is no such thing as a perfect marriage. Why? Because it is a relationship between two imperfect people. I John 1:8 says this clearly and emphatically: *"If we claim to be without sin, we deceive ourselves and the truth is not in us."*

The difficulties may be loud and angry, or they may be quiet and even somewhat hidden, but the question is not "Do we hurt each other?" Rather, the question is "When, and how, and how much do we hurt each other, and what do we do about it?"

Identifying the hurt is the first part in the process of emptying an emotional cup filled with negative feelings of hurt, anger, fear and guilt.

If we can empty these painful emotions many of our symptoms will be dealt with.
Guilt is emptied through confession.
Anger and bitterness through forgiveness.

Accepting responsibility

Many of us find that it is a lot easier to focus on someone else's faults rather than on our own. Jesus refers to this in Matthew 7:1-15 when he asks how can someone see well enough to remove a splinter from another's eye whilst there is a log in their own. Listing hurts done to us may have been a lot easier than listing ways in which a partner has been hurt. Even when it is clear that there has been a wrong done which resulted in pain for our partner, we can resist taking responsibility for the action and try to justify or rationalise what has happened. This response will not bring healing.

In order for forgiveness and healing to take place, each partner must come to realise and feel the other's pain.

Confession of hurts

(Use the following pages as a guide but it may be preferable to work on additional pieces of paper)

James 5:16
"Confess your sins to each other and pray for each other, so that you may be healed".

1. Choose one of the main hurts from the list that your spouse is aware of.

I hurt my husband/wife by ____________________

____

____

2. Try to view this hurt from your husband's / wife's perspective.
Don't excuse yourself, avoid responsibility or blame your husband/wife.

When I hurt my husband/wife in this way, he/she probably felt ____________________

____

____

e.g. sad, upset, discouraged, lonely, unappreciated, disrespected, invisible, unimportant, afraid, wounded, put down, ashamed, abandoned, used.

3. Your husband/wife is in pain. Do you care?

What feelings do you have for your spouse as you consider how you contributed to his/her pain? ____________________

____

____

e.g. sad, regretful, remorse, pain, sorrowful, upset, deeply concerned.
It is important to feel something for your spouse. You may be feeling guilty, ashamed, or angry but these are feelings for or about you .

4. Admit to the action / inaction.
What I did was WRONG - full stop
It hurt the other person.
I need to be forgiven by God and by my spouse.

How does God view what I did?

____

____

____

e.g. God sees that I have been non-dependable and insensitive. It was wrong that I wasn't home at 6 when I said I would be and didn't phone even though it was 7.30 before I returned. My lack of respect for someone He loves hurts God - Jesus died on the cross for my wrong doing. I have really hurt my wife. She needs security. When I do this she feels very insecure and unimportant. I need to ask both for God's forgiveness and for my wife to forgive me.

5. Confession means to agree with God about our wrong doing. Ask God to forgive you and read the promise of God's cleansing.
1 John 1:9 says *"If we confess our sins, he is faithful and just and will forgive us our sins and purify us from all unrighteousness."*
Thank Him for forgiving you.

What emotions do you feel now?

____

____

____

e.g. grateful, overwhelmed, loved, accepted, valued.

6. Express to your spouse your feelings of sorrow for the hurt you have caused.
Using words such as *"I really care about you and your feelings and it saddens me that I've hurt you"* will bring about healing.

7. As you finish confessing and sharing, end your confession with a request for forgiveness. Ask your partner directly *"Will you forgive me?"* This question demonstrates a great deal of vulnerability and humility. The question also provides the listening partner with the opportunity to choose to forgive.

Forgiveness

When we have been hurt, we must be careful not to let the pain turn to anger, bitterness or resentment. Forgiveness helps the offending partner but ultimately the one who has been hurt benefits by being freed from those negative emotions.

1. Seek God's help as you respond to your partner's request for forgiveness.

I was hurt when ____

____

____

2. Which need was unmet relative to that hurt?

____

____

____

What I really needed was

____

____

____

3. Sense what God feels about that hurt.
I feel that God cares about my pain. He cares about what happened to me.

I know that He is saddened because ____

____

____

e,g. *He loves me, I am special to Him and He hurts with me when I am wronged. He wants the best for me.*

4. Choose to forgive.
Eph 4 v.32 "*...forgiving each other just as in Christ God forgave you".*

Forgiveness is a choice not a feeling. Even though you choose to forgive you may not feel like doing so.
Forgiveness means "to turn it loose", "to let it go". It is the anger that you are deciding to let go and sometimes, before you are ready to do that, further opportunity is needed for your partner to understand the depth of your pain.
Forgiveness is unconditional, just as God's forgiveness of us is unconditional.

Offering to forgive only if the promise is made "not to do that again" is not offering unconditional forgiveness. Such "forgiveness" involves fear and is not the way God deals with us.

5. Express to God your forgiveness.

____

____

____

e.g.. *Lord - I was hurt when my husband contradicted me in front of the children. I needed his respect and I felt hurt and angry that I didn't receive it. I know what it is to be forgiven. With your strength and in Jesus' name, I choose to forgive my husband for this disrespect. I choose not to hold onto my anger. I let it go. I won't hold this against him any longer, or expect him to make up for this in some way. I ask for your comfort and healing.*

6. When you make the choice to forgive, reach over and touch your spouse and verbalise your forgiveness by actually saying "I forgive you". Your partner needs to hear the words to help them receive your forgiveness, just as you need to say them in order to seal your decision to forgive. Each entry on the confession list will need to be confessed and forgiven.

7. Dealing With Additional Hurts
Both may now want to ask "*Are there any major hurts I've not seen that need my apology? Please share them with me so that I can confess them now and seek your forgiveness".*

8. After each partner gives and receives forgiveness, destroy the lists. Read James 5:16 together. *"Therefore confess your sins to each other and pray for each other so that you might be healed. The prayer of a righteous man is powerful and effective".*

A Good Habit

"Let not the sun go down on your anger" Eph 4:26

Confession to God and others of hurt we have caused, along with forgiveness of others who have hurt us, must become a daily habit, otherwise our Emotional Cup begins to fill again with hurtful emotions.

Comfort for a marital hurt

Words need to be spoken humbly and sincerely. No excuses, rationalising, explanations, minimising of the other's hurt, or blaming.
The tone of voice needs to communicate "I really care about you and your feelings" and "it saddens me that I have hurt you".
This helps bring about healing of the pain.

What if having forgiven, the pain is still felt?

Another process in emptying the emotional cup of negative emotions is the healing power of comforting.

e.g. I am now aware how my lack of sensitivity to your feelings has hurt you when I don't let you know I shall be late home. I have done this many times. I have been very insensitive to your feelings. You shouldn't have to worry about where I am and if I'm alright. I am deeply sorry that I have put you through all that. My insensitivity and lack of dependability hurts you and it hurts God. I see how it contributes to your insecurity - will you forgive me?

Scatter and share

This is an opportunity to confess and forgive each other for one or more of the hurts already identified. Go through again together all the stages needed for forgiveness to be offered and received. Comfort one another.

"Forgetting what lies behind and pressing forward to what lies ahead" Phil 3 : 13
Focus on the new memory of forgiveness.
Hold hands and pray (even silently) thanking God for His forgiving you, changing you and healing your relationship.

Return to the group

Read together Ephesians 4:31 & 32 ***"Get rid of all bitterness, rage and anger, brawling and slander, along with every form of malice. Be kind to one another forgiving each other, just as in Christ God forgave you."***

Reflecting on hurts may have brought up issues between you that you would appreciate talking over with the course leaders. If so, you are encouraged to take opportunity to arrange a time for this before the next session.

Prayer

Thank you God for your forgiveness and comfort. I commit myself to my partner before You to confess hurt caused, and to forgive hurts received, and to give comfort. Thank you God for the experience of drawing closer to my partner as these hurts, deliberate and unintentional, are healed.

Scatter and Share / Marriage Staff Meeting

You will only begin covering what may need to be dealt with during this session and you should plan for an additional 2 hours of uninterrupted time if you can.

1. In addition to any calendar co-ordination, planning, goal evaluation, you will be seeking to heal the emotional hurts that may have been accumulating in your "emotional cups" for some time now. This is one of your most important "staff meetings". Some guidelines:

a) Both spouses should have prepared for this meeting by completing I. and II. of the "Healing Emotional Hurts" process. Both should bring their two lists.

b) We suggest that the husband begin the process of going through III., IV., and V..

2. One by one, confess each wrong which hurt your partner. (If you are not clear what to do, refer back to the "How to Respond To Your Spouse's urts" worksheet.)

3. After each wrong is confessed, forgiveness should be requested. Wives should then verbalise their decision to actually forgive by saying "I forgive you." Husbands need to hear the words in order to help receive the forgiveness, and wives need to say them in order to seal their choice to forgive.

4. After the husband has completed confessing and asking for forgiveness, an option is to vulnerably ask his wife, "Are there any other ways in which I have hurt you that I have not yet confessed? I'd really like to know, because I care about your hurt." Then respond to anything else that is shared.

5. Husbands should close their portion of the time by praying according to James 5:16, that God would heal the hurt inflicted by the husband's wrong doing.

6. Wives should then proceed in like manner.

7. Husbands and wives should especially remember :

Both comfort and confession are crucial responses to someone else's pain: We must always comfort! We also need to confess if our partner's pain is associated with us!

Blending Four Ingredients for Marriage Intimacy

As you experienced the time of confession and forgiveness arising out of the last session, you may have been able to pray with one another in a new way. Acknowledging wrong, asking for forgiveness and expressing willingness to change knowing that not only God but also your husband/wife is hearing, has been described as vulnerable praying. It's rather different from praying that God will change your husband/wife, by using prayer to give him/her the nudge as to the area they should be doing something about! It's a lot harder to ask for change in ourselves than in our partner. Such vulnerable praying is very effective in increasing closeness in the area of spiritual intimacy.

Knowing our partner's needs, being open to hear exactly what he/she felt during the painful time when hurt was caused (even when on a scale of 1-10 the hurt she/he feels is rated a 10 when we feel a 1 would be a more realistic measure), offering to share our hurts, our fears and our inmost thoughts with our partner, giving and receiving comfort; all of these increase our emotional intimacy.

Intimacy Principles Becoming A Way Of Life

Recapping over the basic principles.
What do we need? Identifying our top three needs.
Be aware of your own and those of your husband/wife. Choose from:

☐	**Approval**	☐
☐	**Attention**	☐
☐	**Affection**	☐
☐	**Acceptance**	☐
☐	**Appreciation**	☐
☐	**Encouragement**	☐
☐	**Comfort**	☐
☐	**Respect**	☐
☐	**Security**	☐
☐	**Support**	☐

Have these needs changed recently?
How are we meeting these needs in each other?
Point out and say "thank you" for times when a particular need has been met.

Four Basic Ingredients for marital closeness.

One of the misconceptions about marriage that exists today, as relationships are increasingly seen as temporary rather than for life, is the marriage myth. This states that a marriage either works or it doesn't. You are either compatible or you are not. Love should be spontaneous and if you don't have those feelings any more then recognise it's all over and find someone else for whom you do have those feelings. Much pain has been borne by those who have tried to respond to that myth.

Intimacy doesn't just happen - it requires some thought and effort. The fact that it does take some effort is not a sign that this is a bad or failing marriage. The truth is that the best marriages are those which have time and attention paid to them, i.e. those which are continually being worked at.

1) Affectionate caring

Affectionate caring says "I care about you". Caring involves reassuring your partner and showing fondness, concern and attentiveness.
You show you care about your spouse when you give your undivided attention when he/she is talking, make giving affection a priority, promise to pray for your partner when he/she is facing a problem. Care can be expressed in a note, phone-call, hug, meal together............

Jesus showed the caring nature of his love when ***"He poured water into the basin and began to wash the disciples' feet".*** John 13:5
We read in 1 Peter 5:7 ***"Cast all your anxiety on him because he cares for you".***
A relationship without care will go stale. Hurts will escalate. Knowing how our partner feels cared for, what makes him/her feel loved, will help us ensure those are the things they receive from us. The simplest gestures may be the most meaningful but they can easily be forgotten. Our goal should be to affectionately care for our spouses in ways that they enjoy even when such ways would not be our own preference .

Think about your relationship and complete the following

I feel cared about by you when

____

____

____

and also when

Being able to show care to another can be hindered by anger, bitterness or resentment. These can hinder our caring for our husband/wife.

My caring feelings for you have been hindered by

e.g. anger when you are suspicious of my motives, bitterness when you don't seem to appreciate my caring expressions, resentment when you belittle my caring gestures.

These hindrances indicate unhealed hurt. Affectionate caring involves positive emotions - the sense of liking each other, being glad about being married, being grateful for our partner.
There is little room for positive emotions when our emotional cup is full of hurt and anger. The process of confession, forgiveness, and comfort will heal hurt and leave room for loving care. We are reminded here of the importance of "emptying of the cup " regularly.

2) Vulnerable Communication says "I trust you"

What do you look most for in a friend?

Many of you will have thought of trust. This is a great quality. When we trust we risk being open about our feelings, needs and hurts.
You can show trust in your spouse when you confide feelings about work problems, share your hopes and dreams, tell him/her what is enjoyable (or not enjoyable) about your sexual times together.

Jesus demonstrated that he trusted his disciples as we read in John 15:15 ***"I have called you friends, for all things that I have heard from my Father I have made known to you".***

Trust says "I appreciate you." It gives permission to talk about the most difficult, personal things without fear of ridicule or indifference. Trusting another means sharing rather than hiding feelings.

Reflect on your relationship with your spouse and complete the following:

I could be more open with my spouse about

____

____

____

e.g. fear that I'm not coping well enough at work, worries that I'm not attractive, anxieties about the effect my lack of patience could be having on the children.

I could be more vulnerable with my spouse by sharing

____

____

____

e.g. *about the difficulty I have responding sexually after my husband/wife has said certain things, hurt I feel when we don't share household tasks, my loneliness even when we are together.*

Fear is a hindrance to trust. Think about the fears that have kept you from being more open and vulnerable with your spouse.

Sometimes I have not been open or vulnerable with my feelings or needs because I fear

____

____

____

e.g. that my husband/wife will ridicule me, I'll look weak or foolish, my spouse will be disappointed in me, my husband/wife will hear it only as a criticism of them and react with anger.

Caring for my marital partner's fear

It is love that casts out fear. We can minister to our partner's fear by assuring him/her of our love. Affectionate caring is the foundation upon which vulnerable communication can be built. If I feel cared for by you I'll be more likely to trust you with vulnerable communication.

3) Joint Accomplishment says "I need you"

A husband/wife who is self-reliant will say to their partner in words or actions "I don't need you". Self-reliance removes closeness and gets in the way of experiencing abundant love.

Closeness comes from enjoying specific activities together. It may include developing common interests, or setting and completing family or house-hold goals.

Jesus talks of the importance of needing each other in John 15:5 ***"I am the vine; you are the branches. If a man remains in me and I in him, he will bear much fruit; apart from me you can do nothing."***

Think about your relationship with your spouse and complete the following:
Together with my husband/wife I would enjoy

I would also enjoy

e.g. learning to play squash, redesigning the garden, losing some weight, redecorating our bedroom, clearing the loft for a car boot sale.............

Needing your spouse alongside and enjoying joint accomplishments can be hindered by an attitude of self sufficiency, fear of failure when trying something new, a critical attitude towards a partner's attempts at a new skill, being a perfectionist.

Think about those things that hinder you from saying "I need you".

I find myself resisting sharing tasks with my partner because of

e.g. I fear rejection or failure, I like to handle things myself...........

4) Mutual Giving says "I love you"

A relationship based upon two people thinking more highly of each other than of themselves characterises mutual giving. A marriage between two people thinking only of taking from the relationship rather than giving to each other will be seriously weakened.

We read in John 15:13 ***"Greater love has no one than this that he lay down his life for his friends."*** Jesus gave His life for us and showed the tremendous depth of his love in His death. John 13:34 calls for our response. ***"A new commandment I give to you that you love one another as I have loved you".***

Within a marriage where mutual giving is happening, love will be given and love will be received.

Reflect upon your relationship with your spouse. One way I could give to my husband/wife would be to

____

____

____

e.g. arrange for him/her to have an evening with friends by taking care of the babysitting, go to watch him/her play sport, getting up to see to the children at night, cooking a favourite meal, surprise him/her with a gift.

The things we say to one another can also give love. One way I can demonstrate how important my husband/wife is to me is by

____

____

____

e.g. praising him/her in front of others, appreciating him/her for special personality qualities, showing how much time spent together alone is precious.

Selfishness can be the major hindrance to giving. Consider ways you may tend to be selfish in your relationship with your marriage partner.

I am sometimes insensitive to my partner's need for

____

____

____

e.g. time alone, opportunity to pursue hobbies, more non-sexual touch, sexual intimacy to be initiated.

I am hindered in giving to my spouse because of my selfishness in

____

____

____

e.g. wanting the last word, wanting my own way, undervaluing things that mean a lot to him/her .

Right Priorities - - Key to Experiencing the Four Ingredients

Blending the four ingredients of caring, trusting, needing and giving into your marriage relationship can bring deeper love and greater happiness.

God says to husbands: "Love your wife as Christ loved the church, and gave Himself up for her..." (Ephesians 5:25).

After directing all of us to "submit toone another out of reverance for Christ," (Ephesians 5:21). He says to wives to submit to husbands as the Lord, prioritizing them as they prioritise the Lord. (Ephesians 5:22)

The priority we give to the things that are important to us can convey a message to our spouse about how much we care, trust, have need of, and are able to give to him/her. Consider now both what you feel your partner's priorities to be and what you would prefer them to be.

What I perceive your top Five priorities to be:

1. ______________________________

2. ______________________________

3. ______________________________

4. ______________________________

5. ______________________________

What I'd love your top Five priorities to be:

1. ______________________________

2. ______________________________

3. ______________________________

4. ______________________________

5. ______________________________

During your Marriage Staff Meeing (or another time):

1. Express to each other: "I desire to help you experience being my top earthly priority."

2. Ask each other: "What would it 'look like' for me to prioritise you and our relationship?"

Scatter and Share

Talk together about your insights into the four ingredients, affectionate caring, vulnerable communication, joint accomplishment, and mutual giving. The order of caring, trusting, needing and giving tends to flow from one to the other. In other words it's hard to trust if I don't sense that you care. It's hard to let you know I need you if I'm not sure I can trust you. It's hard to be motivated to give if I don't sense you really need me.

Spend time discussing the four hindrances to the intimacy ingredients – unresolved anger, fear, self-sufficiency and selfishness. Talk about which causes you the greatest inner turmoil.

Share together these Bible verses:

Eph 4:13
1John 4:18-19
Gal 6:2
Phil 4:19

Reflect together on how experiencing these Bible verses in our lives helps overcome the four hindrances to intimacy.

Talk about your top priorities and recognise and heal hurts caused when priorities have conveyed disregard for your husband/wife.

"Perfect Love" Praying

Consider answering the following question as you reflect on how you could better express love to your spouse:

I want to be more ___________ and less ___________ toward my spouse.

e.g. more sensitive, supportive, affectionant, forgiving, less critical, negative, etc.

Now take turns praying vulmerably together:

Heavenly Father, change me so I can better express love to ___________; make me more___________, and less___________. I don't want to continue hurting him/her. Change me Lord; I want to better love my spouse.

Remember to make time this coming week to finish discussing anything not covered this session.

Express appreciation to each other whenever needs are met. This also helps to reinforce the giving habit.

Return to the Group

Pray about those issues raised tonight such as selfishness, criticism, neglect. Ask for greater sensitivity towards your husband/wife and recognition of changes that need to be made.

Scatter and Share / Marriage Staff Meeting:

In addition to any calendar co-ordination, planning, goal evaluation you need to do,

1. Using the handout or the Keeping Marriages Healthy workbooks share how you completed each sentence for each Intimacy Ingredient.

2. Give each other honest, loving feedback.

3. For example: Yes, I would feel cared for if you gave me a back rub before bed. Or, I would appreciate your prayers that I wouldn't be so afraid to open up, but I think it might help me even more if you could reassure me that you won't make fun of, or put down, what I share with you. Or, I think that our unhealed hurt is still getting in the way of our caring for each other. I think it would be good to set aside some time to work further on confessing to and forgiving each other. When do you think we might plan for this?

4. Share any new insights you discovered regarding the hindrances to the Intimacy Ingredients.

For example: I realised that my selfishness about demanding time alone at the weekend keeps me from enjoying fun times with you and the children.

5. Review with each other the Bible verses to help overcome the hindrances to intimacy.

6. Complete this sentence: "What God most wants to change in me is...

---

7. Hold hands and pray together. Husbands take the lead, followed by wives. Specifically ask God to begin to make the change you identified in No 6. Your prayer might sound something like:

> Dear Heavenly Father, I know that you want me to quickly admit when I am wrong, both to You and to my wife, instead of putting the blame on her. Help me to humble myself, seeing my sin clearly and experiencing your forgiveness. Help me then to confess to my wife, seeking her forgiveness. I want us not to have any unhealed hurt between us so that we can be free to affectionately care for each other. In Jesus' name, Amen.

The Family Tree

"For this reason a man shall leave father and mother, cleave to his wife, and the two shall become one flesh" Genesis 2:24

So far the emphasis has been upon ways in which we can draw closer as a couple and concentrating upon hindrances within the marriage to that closeness growing. We have seen that the inevitable hurts of marriage need to be healed. Regularly confessing our wrongs to each other, forgiving each other, and giving comfort, can become the standard for our marriage. We benefit from needs being expressed in a positive loving way. Mutually giving to meet each other's needs will deepen satisfaction and happiness.

Within the security of a relationship in which these things are experienced, we are able to turn to look at hurts received from elsewhere and in particular from our past. We are reassured that we will be dealing with our past with our spouse. We will not be alone.

Taking a look back

In many of us there is a resistance to look back. Some will feel that what is past is past, why dredge it up? Be reassured that only past events which require attention, resolving, and healing need to be addressed. No suggestion is made to look back just for the sake of it.

Others may say "my past isn't affecting me" and therefore there is no need to look back. We will be exploring further how we are affected by past events.

Another response can be "It doesn't matter any way". Jesus calls us to live life abundantly and one of the greatest barriers to living life that way can be unhealed hurt. You are precious and valued and worth any healing that can take place. It is sometimes those with the most pain from childhood, who have little self worth, who need some convincing that they matter enough.

An anxiety about dishonouring parents and in particular criticising a loved parent who has now died, can also cause us not to want to identify any hurts from childhood. Again the goal is not to blame, accuse or criticise. In fact the Bible asks us to honour our parents. However, just as in marriage hurts will be inevitably received, often unintentionally, so parents will make mistakes, choose the wrong options, cause their much loved children pain by missing a particular need. The Bible asks us to honour our parents but also to "leave" them. Inviting our spouse to comfort and heal hurts from childhood, helping to "remove our aloneness" during that time by their comfort now, will help fulfil the verse from Genesis about "leaving and cleaving".

Identifying three things that need to be left.

On the day of a couple's wedding there is much anticipation and excitement about the future. As the ceremony ends and they turn to face family and friends as husband and wife, thoughts are directed to the new life they are starting together. That is perhaps not the time to be thinking about anything except what lies ahead. However, once the early days of married life begin it may soon become very clear that each has brought a lot of "baggage" into the relationship.
The baggage may include several things.

1. Beliefs

This includes the expectations we have of our marriage. How are we going to sort out our roles in this relationship? There may be the view that women do certain jobs around the house and men others e.g. *who takes the rubbish out, who locks up at night, who drives the car on long journeys, who cleans the bathroom, checks the oil in the car.............*
There are no right or wrong answers on these issues but there may be very strong views often related to our experiences in our childhood home.

Some of these views will need to be left particularly when, for example, the association is made between love being given and a particular role being fulfilled; e.g. a husband shows love by putting the dustbin out!

Messages such as "look after yourself, no one else will" can be another thought we bring into our marriage as part of our beliefs. We may not even realise other families don't share or practise that view. Thinking patterns are also another aspect of this. We look in a later session at thinking patterns that can damage healthy relationships. Most of the thinking that shapes our marriage was learnt at home in childhood.

2. Behaviour

Patterns of behaviour are also learnt in childhood. How we deal with conflict is a good example of this. Some will always want to win, others avoid conflict at all costs, others seek compromise whenever possible.

Another example concerns the way in which affection is given and received. Some feel affection when things are bought or when they are taken somewhere special, for others a hug or a cuddle is more important.

A husband or wife may have experienced "games" being played, when communication failed. Instead of needs being vulnerably expressed, attempts would be made to seek attention for example by the "nothing is wrong game". Denial of anything being the matter is accompanied by tone of voice and facial and body expression making clear the opposite is true. Attention is received and care shown only because one takes from the other. The more that denial of a problem is maintained the more the other partner persists with enquiries about what really is the matter and the more excluded he/she feels from the partner's "world". Such attention isn't satisfying but that is the game played out many times.

Behaviour patterns are learned at home and may be carried into the marriage relationship. They may also be reacted against so that the behaviour brought into the marriage is in direct contrast to that experienced in childhood.

3. Emotions

Unresolved anger, fears, guilt, shame from childhood and unhealed hurt from unmet needs can also all be brought into those early months and years of marriage. This emotional baggage can affect the quality of our marriage because it affects our thinking, our reactions, our feelings about family life.

"Leaving" then, is going to mean unpacking this baggage from our past, especially from our family. We will identify what we brought into our marriage, be grateful for what is good and helpful and then "leave behind" what is not good, true or helpful.

When we reflect on childhood, what are we looking for?

What might I be grateful for? Have I expressed this gratitude to God and my parents?

Where have my marriage expectations come from? Which need to be left behind?

Which of my actions need to be "left"? What am I reacting to, or over-compensating for, that needs to be "left"?

Do I have hurt which needs to be left behind through expressing it and being comforted?

What needs did I have which went unmet?

Intimacy needs in childhood

Unmet need in childhood could still be influencing your relationships as an adult unless these needs are understood and the losses faced. It is helpful to assess the degree to which intimacy needs were met or not met by your parents / guardians in childhood.

Look at the Intimacy Needs listed next and ask

1. "How did my mother consistently meet this need?" If you can recall specific ways in which she met this need, put a half circle alongside that need on the list. e.g. you may recall her reading stories to you at bedtime which met your need for attention.
2. "How did your father consistently meet this need?" If you can recall specific times and ways your father met this need, put a half circle against that need on the list. e.g. I remember Dad giving me a hug when my bike was stolen.

If only one person met a need you will have a half-circle beside it. If both parents/guardians met the need you will have a full circle.
Place an X against any of the needs that are blank, indicating that those needs were not met consistently by either mother or father.

If your childhood involved carers other than your biological parents due to death, divorce, or adoption then complete the exercise twice first reflecting how your needs were met by biological parents and then by carers. The fact that one or both of your biological parents were not there to meet needs represents a loss that may still need to be grieved.

Intimacy Needs Met ( ) or unmet X in childhood

Acceptance - deliberate and favourable reception/response ☐

Affection - loving care communicated verbally/appropriate touch ☐

Appreciation - communicating personal gratefulness for another ☐

Approval - to think and speak well of, to praise ☐

Attention - to take thought of another, to enter into another's world ☐

Comfort- to come alongside with tenderness and consolation ☐

Encouragement - to urge forward towards a goal in a positive way ☐

Respect - to value and regard highly; to convey great worth ☐

Security - confidence of harmony in relationship; free from harm/fear ☐

Support - to come alongside and gently carry a load ☐

Performance Pressure

How would you finish these sentences?

1. Love becomes conditional when I withhold affection because my spouse has not

___

___

___

e.g. agreed with my point of view, spontaneously noticed I'm feeling down, come home early from work, put petrol in the car, arranged an evening out for a special occasion....

2. I sometimes feel performance pressure concerning

___

___

___

e.g. keeping on top of the housework, lovemaking, seeking promotion...........

3. I sometimes find myself pressurising my spouse about

___

___

___

e.g. helping around the house, spending time with the children, how frequently we make love

4. Some of my "pressure tactics" include

___

___

___

e.g. nagging and complaining, becoming remote and withdrawn, saying no to sex, comparing with a friend, sibling, neighbour

Completing the Childhood Questionnaire

Reflect on Childhood Memories:

When you were married you began to unpack them!

You brought both the good and the bad stuff with you.

What were the unmet needs you brought into your marriage?

One of the most destructive things parents can heap upon their children is the pressure to perform in order to be loved. It's unfair pressure, but it's also often pressure given without even thinking about it. Expecting or demanding that another person perform in certain ways to merit acceptance, approval, and love is a key ingredient in *unhealthy* relationships.

Performance pressure is contagious.

A child unknowingly can easily begin to believe that

Performance = Love

Performance pressure/demands might look like any of the below

- a parent's consistent focus on a child's lowest grade in school
- a parent constantly asking "Is that the best you can do?"
- emphasis on what is not done, not complete, and not sufficient rather than simply praising the child's progress
- verbal put-downs that attack the child's worth or character
- derogatory nicknames
- comparisons with others who are seemingly more perfect
- not tolerating normal emotional expressions of hurt, sadness, and anger
- any form of abuse - physical, emotional, or sexual
- expectations to be just like Mum or Dad
- pressure not to cause problems for your parents like a rebellious sibling did

Referring to the above list, write your answers to the following:

1. Growing up in my family, I sometimes felt like I needed to measure up to....

___

___

___

e.g. Mum's expectations about my looks, sister's/brother's achievements, Dad's plans for my future, society pressure as to my role as a man/woman............

2. When I was growing up I received praise for

___

___

___

e.g. good marks and exam results, looking attractive, playing sports, winning at sports, my honesty, working around the house......

Look at your list. Are most of the things you were praised for as a child related to things you DID, or was the praise focused on WHO YOU ARE AS A PERSON?

Write down any thoughts you may have about this.

Looking back at your childhood are there any messages you received from your parents that seem inappropriate?

e.g. *real men don't cry, being fat is unacceptable, I must always do the best, I must always be the best, you can do better next time.....*

Are there any ways in which those messages have affected your marriage?

The Neglectful Home

In this environment parents are under-involved with their children in meaningful ways. Neglect may be present for different reasons; alcoholic or workaholic homes, parents preoccupied, distant, emotionally closed. The message received is "You're just not important to me".

A child might seek attention through achieving well at school or sport, or through disruptive behaviour or inappropriate ways of achieving popularity with peers.

Jot down some thoughts about any experience of under-involved parents.

As a child I tried to get attention or to be noticed by...

Drawing from childhood memories list one-word, or one-phrase descriptions for each of your parents.

e.g. hard working, easy to talk to, fun, honest

e.g. perfectionist, easily angered rigid, self reliant

FATHER

Strengths

Weaknesses

MOTHER

Strengths

Weaknesses

What things did you like about yourself when you were a child?

e.g. I was good at sport, I had lots of friends, I was good with animals, I could make people laugh, I was sensitive ....

What things did you like least about yourself when you were a child?

e.g. *I wasn't clever at school, I was often left out, I was fat, I was easily bullied ..*

When you were a child, how would mum praise you?

criticise you?

When you were a child, how would dad praise you?

criticise you?

As you grew up how did you know that mum loved you?

e.g .*she would tell me, she hugged me, she bought me things, she did things for me ......*

As you grew up how did you know that dad loved you?

How did mum and dad deal with conflict between themselves? with you?
Dad would

Mum would

How did you know your parents loved each other as you were growing up?

How did they show it?

e.g. *they hugged and kissed a lot, they just got on well, they laughed a lot, they gave each other space................*

Indicate either "Mum" "Dad", "Both" "Neither" next to the following phrases to help describe your life as a child:

- Family Leader ________________
- Main Disciplinarian____________
- Quick Temper_________________
- Comfortable giving affection to me_________________________
- Hard to please_______________
- Parent I felt closest to___________________________

What best describes your thoughts of your childhood?

- Our family appeared normal to everyone else - but wasn't
- I was cared about because of the things I did
- I was loved for who I was -- my character
- I was kind of an outsider, an observer of the rest of the family
- Our home was demanding, performance-based, lots of rules
- I often felt alone
- I always felt like we "walked on egg shells" around our home
- It was always important for me to please everyone
- I'm not sure that anyone knew the "real" me

Reflecting on your family, do you think anything was missing from your family: If so what?

____

____

____

How did you feel as you were completing the above questions?

____

____

____

Do you think your experiences as a child may be affecting how you relate to your marriage partner?

____

____

____

e.g. I don't take suggestions easily because it reminds me of my controlling mother, I need a lot of attention now because I missed it from my father, I am over-sensitive to criticism because of the teasing I received,......................

When you were a child who gave you......?

Affection ______________________________________

Comfort ______________________________________

Attention ______________________________________

Scatter and Share

Spend the time beginning to share your responses to the childhood questionnaire with your spouse. Comfort your husband/wife for hurt resulting from unmet need in their childhood.

Remember that comfort involves your feelings for your partner not at the situation that hurt them. Getting angry about the person who hurt them, or rationalising about why it may have happened, will not give comfort.

Whilst you may even have had similar experiences you will each need comfort for the situation you experienced. Comfort will not be received by immediately saying "Yes I had that too".

Whilst hurt and pain need to be dealt with you will also draw closer as a couple if you can rejoice with one another about the good times you experienced.

Emotional Need/Hurt

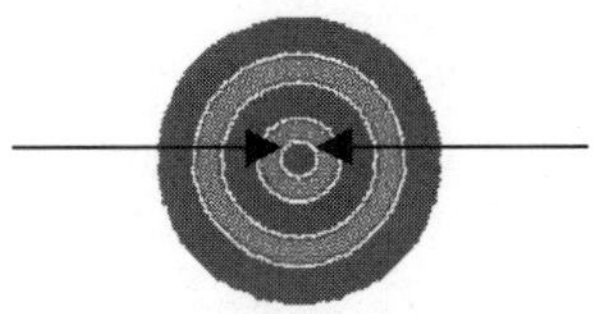

Bringing
"healing" "understanding"
"fulfilment" "closeness"

Emotional Responding

Emotional responding always includes understanding, empathy, gentleness, reassurance and often will include confession.

Examples of Productive Emotional Responses

"I can really see that you are hurting."
"I genuinely regret my part in hurting you"
"I don't like to see you hurting"
"Can you share with me how I hurt you?
"How did it make you feel? I want to understand and make it right"

"I can see that I hurt you by my ….. and that was wrong of me. Will you forgive me?"
"It saddens me to see you so fearful."
"I deeply care about you and love you"
"I'm committed to go through this with you"

"It really saddens me that you missed ____________________.
It hurts me that ________________________ because I care about you; I love you."

Return to the Group

Pray for continued healing of hurtful childhood experiences. Give thanks to God for the positive experiences that each has had. As you hold hands together thank God that he has brought you together and for the special way you can minister to each other now.

Scatter and Share / Marriage Staff Meeting

1. In addition to any calendar co-ordination, planning, and goal evaluation you need to do, each spouse should complete the Childhood Questionnaire.

2. Sharing the completed Childhood Questionnaire with each other will take time, and priority needs to be given to listening and responding appropriately to each other.

3. Reflecting upon needs, both well met and unmet in each other's past will give insight into each other's needs now. It will be helpful to be particularly attentive to meeting each other's priority needs this coming week.

4. Remember to plan some shared activities.

5. Take opportunity to verbalise appreciation for each other.

6. Affirming each other in affection will also build security.

7. Pray for each other.

Break Free From Unhealthy Thinking

As we thought about our childhood families, it became clear that whilst parents' motives for their children can be good, the methods they choose can be hurtful. A parent can want the best for a child they deeply love, but the way they go about achieving that may not be appropriate.

A parent may long that their child has opportunities they missed themselves e.g. learning a musical instrument. The child however may feel no choice about the lessons and the practice needed, and begin to resent the opportunity. The parent's motive was good but the method not helpful.

Thinking Patterns

A thinking pattern is the habitual way our minds process what is happening to us and around us. Some of our thinking patterns are good and healthy, reflecting what is true. Some are not good. Some may reflect significant distortions of truth which hinder our ability to handle life and experience intimacy in our relationships. We may have seen certain ways of thinking modelled by parents. We need to ask, whether our mental habit patterns reflect the truth.

Six unhealthy, distorted patterns will be identified and opportunity given to explore whether we are prone to any. Faulty thinking needs to be challenged and replaced with truth. Our pattern of thinking about the things that happen to us can add to our pain.

Unhealthy Thinking Questionnaire

Review the statements and indicate agreement or disagreement for yourself and then for your spouse. In other words are the statements true for you? Are the statements seem true for your spouse?

Myself Agree/disagree			Spouse Agree/disagree
_______	1.	I see things very much as black and white.	_______
_______	2.	I tend to make mountains out of mole-hills.	_______
_______	3.	I often take things personally.	_______
_______	4.	Past disappointments seem to predict the future.	_______
_______	5.	What I am feeling is more important than the facts.	_______
_______	6.	I often think people make too much of their problems. They should just get over it.	_______
_______	7.	There is a place for everything and everything in its place.	_______
_______	8.	Everything seems a major issue.	_______
_______	9.	It's very important to sense others' approval.	_______
_______	10.	I just know things won't get any better.	_______
_______	11.	I can't really believe I'm loved unless I feel it.	_______
_______	12.	I can handle almost any problem that comes my way. I don't really need much support from anyone.	_______
_______	13.	Being perfect in what I undertake is essential to me.	_______
_______	14.	I seem to over-react to relatively small irritations.	_______
_______	15.	If someone in my family is upset, I must have been part of the reason.	_______
_______	16.	I tend to write people off if they hurt or disappoint me.	_______
_______	17.	If I feel unloved, it must be because no one loves me.	_______
_______	18.	There's no reason to get so worked up or so emotional.	_______

Now look over each of the statements that were true for you. The chart below gives the questions that match the six unhealthy patterns. Find the items that you agreed with, then identify which thinking pattern(s) the statement represents.

	Polarising	Magnifying	Personalising
Questions	1, 7, 13	2, 8, 14	3, 9, 15
	Generalising	Emotional Reasoning	Minimising
Questions	4, 10, 16	5, 11, 17	6, 12, 18

Our marriage partner may have helpful insights about our own thinking pattern. Their insights may even be more accurate than our own. Listen carefully and non-defensively to your partner's view.

The particular thinking pattern we ought to pay attention to would be our high score, the one ticked off most.
According to this exercise, I have a tendency toward

____

____

____

According to this exercise my spouse seems to have a tendency toward

____

____

____

These unhealthy thinking patterns contribute to emotional pain. Everyone seems to fall victim to at least one of these patterns. When we come to consider ways of overcoming these patterns two Bible verses will be helpful.

2 Cor 10:5 ***"We take captive every thought to make it obedient to Christ"*** and

Phil 4:8 ***"Whatever is true, whatever is noble, whatever is right, whatever is pure, whatever is lovely, whatever is admirable - if anything is excellent or praiseworthy - think about such things"***

1. Polarising:

- Only one way to do something.
- Everything is right or wrong
- See the world in absolutes.

Description

Life viewed as all or nothing, good or bad, black or white. Rigid rules held for evaluating life. Little satisfaction felt in modest performance or genuine effort. Experience little joy when successful, since it was expected all along.

Background

Often brought up in legalistic, critical or performance - orientated families where there were many insecurities and fears. Perhaps whatever the child did was never good enough. Perhaps others around them were consistently criticised and evaluated.

Truth

Some issues are black or white but many are shades of grey. The scriptures encourage discernment, but deciding to hold something against another or myself is "judging" and is warned against (Matthew 7:1-5 and elsewhere). The "middle ground" can often be acceptable and enjoyed (Ephesians 5:20).

Effects within a marriage

Polarisers have a perfectionist thinking pattern and can be more than a little difficult to live with. They may judge their spouse's performance on the basis of their own impossible standards.

Overcoming Polarising

Take note of your reactions and analyse what prompted your response. ***"Take those thoughts captive - cast them down"*** 2 Cor 10:3-5 ***"Think on those things that are true".*** Phil 4:8

e.g. Your project is criticised.
Your reaction is "I knew I'd fail".
The consequence is anger at the critic and at yourself.
If "I knew I'd fail" is replaced with "The project wasn't perfect but there was a lot of good in it. I can improve it" then the renewed response can be to evaluate criticism, consider changes and move on.

Dispute the faulty thinking and practise the new responses with your partner's help and support. One of the most important steps in this process is to be aware of what is happening.

Take Thoughts Captive 2 Corinthians 10:5	**Think About What is True** Philippians 4:8
Replace: (e.g.) "If it's not done this way, it won't work."	With: "My way is not the only way; others' ways may work OK, too."
Replace:	With:
Replace:	With:
Replace:	With:

2. Personalising:

Take external events as personal rejections and attacks.
"My fault" thought pattern.

Description

Overestimates the extent that an event is related to him/her. Tends to be moody and easily hurt by seeming rejections. Often insecure and self-condemned. May blame self for everything. Others may view as fragile, overly sensitive, childish, self-centred even hysterical.

Background

Often were rejected, abused or neglected in childhood or came from a highly critical home environment where he/she was often wrongly blamed for whatever was happening.

Truth

We are not the target or cause of everything that happens to us. Usually what occurs is not aimed at us, or is more a statement about the other person than about us. Biblical truth would include Romans 12:3, Philippians 2:3-4, 1 Peter 5:7.

Effects within a marriage

When we take everything personally we run the risk of overreacting to our spouse and causing unnecessary tensions in marriage.

Overcoming Personalising

Begin by taking notice of incidents when personalising has taken place. It may even be helpful to write them down. You may have strong feelings of anger, upset, hurt. Ask your partner to help you identify the "lies". Practice replacing them (taking thoughts captive) with more rational truthful thinking (think on those things that are true).

e.g. A friend phones to cancel coming for coffee because she needs to visit her mother in hospital.
Your reaction; she probably didn't want to come for coffee anyway.
Consequences of that reaction; you feel rejected, hurt, annoyed and you neglect to show concern for your friend's mother, you may even go on to think "she probably doesn't like me any-way. In fact no one really likes me."

This reaction could be replaced by; I feel disappointed that our cup of coffee together can't take place but my friend must go to her mother. I'll look forward to us being able to rearrange for another day. I wonder how I can support my friend whilst her mother is ill.

Take Thoughts Captive II Corinthians 10:5	**Think About What is True** Philippians 4:8
Replace: (e.g.) "I'm sure it's my fault."	With: "I may have contributed to the problem, but I want to get some more information before I accept total responsibility."
Replace:	With:
Replace:	With:
Replace:	With:

3.Generalising:

Past events become predictors of future.

Description

Believes that past events will always predict the future, generalising from past to future. Whatever has happened before will unavoidably happen again. Nothing will, or even can change including the person. Often lacks initiative and is usually pessimistic.

Background

Often "trained" in this thinking pattern in home environment as it was modelled by one or both parents. May have been given the label fatty, pest, clumsy, thick............

Truth

What has happened before does not have to happen again. If I put in some effort , things can be different and even better.

Effects within a marriage

The attitude may be "No matter what we do we'll never get along with each other".
Generalisers carry around loads of anxiety, doubt and fear. They hold on to past hurts, failures, and rejections and use them as evidence for their gloomy attitude towards the future.
e.g. One argument with a neighbour must mean we will never have anything more to do with them.

Overcoming Generalising

Begin by recognising how often you are giving this message and pinpoint specific examples.
e.g. you eat something not allowed on a new diet,
Your reaction:- I'll never lose weight.
Consequences of the reaction:- stop trying, become self-condemning, may eat even more unhealthily.
Replace with:- I am in control of my eating and I choose whether to eat or not.
With more truthful thinking the response to one day of failure on a new diet will be "I'll begin again now".

Take Thoughts Captive 2 Corinthians 10:5	**Think About What is True** Philippians 4:8
Replace: (e.g.) "I've never had good marks before, why bother? I'll never be a good student."	With: “My low marks before were probably the result of not studying well. I can learn how to study and with effort raise my marks."
Replace:	With:
Replace:	With:
Replace:	With:

4. Magnifying:

Making mountains out of mole-hills.

Description

Exaggerates events until everything seems like a catastrophe. May be volatile with anger, unmerciful with self-condemnation or overwhelmed with fear or self pity. May be viewed as self-absorbed, pre-occupied with one's own crises, whiny and over-reactive.

Background

Often raised in an environment in which little things were blown out of proportion. Spilled milk provoked a character attack; discipline may have been excessive and out of proportion to the offence. Possibly a parent was pre-occupied with loneliness, rejection, or fear, which contributed to them seeing catastrophes in every situation.

Possible indicators of magnifying

Frequent use of extreme words and phrases such as never, every, devastated, worst, ruined, terrible, horrible, awful, beyond repair, too late, all, nothing.

Truth

Mole-hills are not mountains. Not everything is a major event. A 50p event needs a 50p reaction. People sometimes treat us badly, but not always. We do some things wrong, but not everything. It is usually too soon to give up.

Effect upon a marriage

It is hard to live in an atmosphere where every little event is made to feel like a catastrophe. When difficult events do arise there is little ability to cope. Emotional energy is sapped by trying to exist with "big" events.

Overcoming Magnifying

Be alert for the trigger words always, every, no one, never, awful, worst, terrible, horrible. Analyse what caused this sort of response and then take your thoughts captive, replace them with more rational truthful thinking.

e,g. A broken coffee mug:
Your reaction:- that's it, my whole day is ruined!
Consequences of that response:- negative attitude which results in the bad day, anger, depression, self blame.
Replace with:- These things happen, it's just a mug that can easily be replaced. Let's clean it up.

Take Thoughts Captive 2 Corinthians 10:5	**Think About What is True** Philippians 4:8
Replace: (e.g.) "Everything is ruined!"	With: "This situation isn't so good but I can get over it. I wonder how God might be working at the moment?"
Replace:	With:
Replace:	With:

5. Minimising;

Significant events are never dealt with.

Description

Most, if not all, important events are denied or discounted. The person tends not to feel or express emotions, so he/she tends to expect or demand the same from others. Even during life's major events, little emotion is shown. The person denies that anything is wrong or that anything troubles him/her. Much effort may be expended to "put a good face on things". Often is impatient with others who show emotions.

Background

Often comes from homes where personal needs were neglected or overlooked. To cope with pain they "shut down" and acted as if nothing was wrong. May have learned or been encouraged to deny their own needs, which promotes losing touch with their own feelings. May have become self-reliant or self-sufficient. May have seen this pattern modelled by others important to them.

Truth

Some of life's events are major happenings and are worth a significant emotional and/or behavioural response. Jesus came to give abundant life. Pain needs to be mourned and comforted.

Effects within a marriage

Minimisers tend to verbalise few emotions and expect the same from others around them, often leaving spouses lonely, frustrated and feeling hurt, particularly during tragic events when little or no feeling is demonstrated. They deny that anything troubles them and, when pressed to communicate they give facts, opinions, or logical explanation rather than vulnerably sharing their needs and feelings.

Overcoming Minimising

Comfort for the pain of unmet needs may be needed before you are able to recognise that not showing emotion when painful feelings have been experienced is not healthy. Reassurance that showing emotions is not the same as losing control may need to be given by a partner. Trust yourself to verbalising feelings to your partner. Take captive the thought that to show emotion is a sign of weakness and choose the more positive response of becoming aware of how you feel.

Take Thoughts Captive 2 Corinthians 10:5	**Think About What is True** Philippians 4:8
Replace: (e.g.) "This happens to everyone; I'll get over it."	With: "As I feel my pain, grieve the hurt, and receive comfort from God and others, I'll get over it."
Replace:	With:
Replace:	With:
Replace:	With:

6. Emotional Reasoning:

Feelings are interpreted as facts.

Description

Believes that feelings are the equivalent of truth. Feelings are confused with facts. Feelings are also confused with thoughts. A person may say "I just don't feel that you care", which means that since I don't feel your care, the fact is no matter what you say, you don't care. " A more precise statement might be "I don't think you care" or "I'm afraid that you don't care." In this latter statement the real emotion - fear - is honestly expressed.

Background

Person may have suffered deep emotional trauma in childhood, such as physical or sexual abuse. May have frequently felt afraid but didn't receive any help dealing with their fears. May have seen emotional reasoning modelled. May have experienced broken promises, prompting "I'll believe it when I see it".

Truth

Even though I "feel it", it may not be true. Feelings are feelings, no more and no less. They are not facts. When I say "I feel that........." , I'm really expressing a thought and I may be feeling important emotions such as hurt, fear, or anger. If so I need to identify what the real feelings are and then vulnerably express them.

Effects within marriage

Confusing feelings with facts can play havoc with a marriage. Accusations can fly about based not on any evidence only a feeling. e.g. I feel jealous therefore my husband/ wife must be having an affair. Such a home will be dominated by fear and mistrust. The partner becomes very frustrated.

Overcoming "Emotional Reasoning"

Accept the truth that feelings have their place but they can't take the place of truth. Notice incidents when emotional reasoning has been allowed to take over. Allow your partner to talk about this with you. Take wrong thoughts captive and think about true responses.

e.g. your partner is late home:
Your reaction:- I just know he/she is with someone else.
Consequences of the reaction:- accusing, attacking, angry, resentful.
Replace with:- there is probably a good reason for their delay.
With more truthful thinking the response to your partner when they return can be, "I get very concerned when you are late and get fearful about the reason for your delay."

Take Thoughts Captive 2I Corinthians 10:5	**Think About What is True** Philippians 4:8
Replace: (e.g.) "That's just how I feel."	With: "My feelings are important, but they may not be consistent with truth. I need to live according to truth, even if my feelings don't yet line up."
Replace:	With:
Replace:	With:

A Comparison

John Smith has worked for a company for the past three years. He has just received notice that due to a down-turn in the economy, the company will be laying off 400 employees, and he's one of them. What kind of thinking might John have in response to this news?

If he "**polarises**":
"So that's the decision—redundancies. Well, this company is obviously going down the drain. If they don't want me, then I certainly don't want them!"

If he "**magnifies**":
"This is the worst thing that could possibly happen! My life is over! I'm ruined. What am I going to do?"

If he "**personalises**":
"I knew my boss didn't like me. He's been waiting for a chance to get rid of me. What did I do wrong?"

If he "**generalises**":
"This was bound to happen sooner or later. Big companies never care anything about their employees. This always seems to happen to me--I'll never keep a steady job."

If he "**emotionally reasons**":
"Don't talk to me about economic down-turns--I just feel like there's something else going on here. It feels like they are not telling us the whole truth about all this and I'm really angry about it."

If he "**minimises**":
"Well it's no big deal, these things happen. No need to even talk about it. What's done is done--not much any of us can do about it."

Breaking free

It is important to recognise which patterns we struggle with. One of them may stand out or there may be parts of several taking root. Admitting to our marriage partner that we recognise a tendency to think in a certain way, and asking for support in overcoming the unhealthy reaction and seeing the truth, is an excellent start. It is very hard to correct alone.

You may have recognised one thinking pattern for yourself and another for your spouse. Sometimes the combination can create particular stresses. A minimiser and a magnifier living together can be very frustrating for example.

A gentle, understanding, comforting response by one partner to the other will bring the change that a negative critical complaining approach will not. Be ready to recognise that overcoming unhealthy thinking is a struggle which requires support and understanding.

Scatter and Share

Talk about the issues raised in this session and exchange insights that the unhealthy thinking questionnaire has given.
Recognise any tendency for you to have two different, clashing thinking patterns.
Discuss the most helpful ways you can show support to each other in overcoming wrong reactions.
Comfort one another for the pain experienced because of unhealthy reactions, and confess and forgive each other for the ways those responses have harmed your marriage.

Remember to make time this week for a Marriage Staff Meeting to finish this.

Return to group

Read together 1 Cor. 13:4-13

Pray together asking that God will strengthen your love for one another. Focus on one description of love from this passage that you would particularly like to show more of towards your marriage partner. Thank God for the love you receive.

Scatter and Share/Marriage Staff Meeting

In addition to any calendar co-ordination, planning, confessing and forgiving, or goal evaluation you need to do, set aside at least one hour to:

1. Husbands, begin by sharing with your partner the one or two faulty thinking patterns you would most like to see changed in yourself: "I realise that I have a problem with____________________. I'd really like the Lord to help me change this."

2. Then share the particular "untruths" that you will seek to "dispute". Also, share the truths you will strive to replace them with.

3. Wives, do the same.

4. Talk about some of the childhood experiences that may have contributed to these thinking patterns. How did you observe these patterns in your own family? What did you experience which may have prompted your faulty thinking patterns? Do any of the possibilities described in the "Background" section for your thinking patterns "ring true?"

If there are any painful memories which begin to be expressed, let the feelings come out. Express them and receive your partner's comfort. Partners, remember to emotionally respond to any expressions of hurt and sadness.

5. Ask for your partner's assistance in overcoming the self deceptions associated with these thinking patterns. Be sure to tell your partner how he/she can best help you. What would you want your partner to say to you? How would you want your partner to say it?

Example: "When I am magnifying – overreacting to something - I think I'd like you to approach me this way: '(Spouse name), I'm sensing that you may be reacting a little out of proportion to what's happening at the moment. Is there something I can do to help you now?' I think that might help me."

6. Close your time by praying for yourself that God would give you His truth and the ability to take any lies captive to the obedience of Christ. Pray specifically that God would enable you to overcome the particular faulty thinking pattern that you struggle with.

Intimacy Becoming a Way of Life

Becoming Friends, Lovers and Saints.

I Tim 4:7 ***"......train yourself to be godly. For physical training is of some value, but godliness has value for all things, holding promise for both the present life and the life to come."***

Intimacy Disciplines

Each of the sessions covered so far has been highlighting certain intimacy disciplines needed for a relationship to benefit and therefore grow. For our marriages to remain healthy certain practices, maybe newly discovered, will need to become a central part of our lives.

Discipline is not a word we are over comfortable with today. Discipline however can be habit forming and it is these new habits we have been discovering that can transform our marriages. We need discipline then, not just for the sake of it, but because it brings growth and increased closeness. For example you should not only be aware that your partner has needs, but know what they are, and be regularly giving attention to them.

Deepening Spiritual Intimacy

Cultivate intimacy with God both individually and together. God bestows His grace on us, and by His grace we respond to His love and share what we receive with others. Because Jesus died and rose again we can live in Him, drawing on His strength, wisdom and love.

Together read some verses of the Bible and then pray, even if it's silently. The Intimate Moments devotional will focus thought for this.

Psalm 103:2 ***"Praise the Lord Oh my soul and forget none of His benefits".***

Thankfulness and gratitude.
Expressing to God thankfulness for all that he has given you will deepen your awareness of His love for you. Gratefulness guards us from a critical negative spirit. It also guards us from being judgmental. Share with one another thankfulness for your friendship with Jesus, His forgiveness, His gift of the Holy Spirit, for the life-changing truth in the Bible.

Confession
I John 1:9 and James 5:16
If too long goes by between times of confession then pain and hurt will accumulate. As we experience the truth of the verses from John and James then healing will take place. Remember to be aware of how long it has been since a time of confession.

Forgiveness
This is the practice of "putting away" anger, pain. In marriage we will be hurt in different ways. There may be the regular disappointment. There can also be the more significant incidents of hurt which bring great pain. Practising the discipline of forgiveness once real confession has taken place will deepen love.

Vulnerable praying
Praying vulnerably to God with your

marriage partner will address fear. Not only can a hurtful deed be confessed and forgiven, but a willingness to change will also be evident.e.g. *Lord, I long to be more sensitive, caring, supportive to ....(my husband/wife); please show me how.* Establishing such praying regularly will be supportive and encouraging.

Comforting
Matt 5:4 ***"Blessed are those who mourn for they shall be comforted".***
The marriage relationship is a source of refuge and security. A place where the door can be closed for a while on the world and where there is comfort rather than criticism or advice. Where pain can be expressed, where there is listening, and where words and touch can bring comfort and healing.

Administer Grace

Ephes 4:29 ***"Do not let any unwholesome talk come out of your mouths, but only what is helpful for building others up according to their needs, that it may benefit those who listen".***
This is about building each other up, appreciating each other. So there is a need to be careful how we speak to each other.

Deepening Friendship Intimacy

Friends make time for each other.
Making a Marriage Staff Meeting a weekly commitment may require a lot of effort at first but this is the key to "Keeping a Marriage Healthy". If time to talk about all the issues covered in this workbook is left to chance, if there is no plan nor goal, then there is a danger of slipping back into bad habits.

Make spending time together a priority, sharing interests, having a romantic meal together, planning a fun time together. These are important.

Friends heal inevitable hurts through comforting, confession and forgiveness.

Friends communicate their needs in loving ways - not critically, not demandingly, not silently, not manipulatively.

Friends express appreciation for each other.

As you look at the following list choose those character qualities that describe your husband/wife. During the Scatter and Share time later express your appreciation for those particular qualities in you partner.

1. Acceptance
Deliberate and ready reception with a favourable response. To receive someone unconditionally and willingly.

2. Cautiousness
Gaining adequate counsel before making decisions. Recognising temptations and fleeing from them.

3. Compassion
Feeling the hurt of others and doing all that is possible to relieve them.

4. Contentment
Enjoying present possessions rather than desiring new or additional ones.

5. Creativity
Finding ways to overcome seemingly impossible obstacles. Discovering practical applications for spiritual principles.

6. Decisiveness
Finalising difficult decisions on the basis of God's ways, Word and will.

7. Deference
Limiting own freedom in order not to offend the personal tastes of those God has called one to serve.

8. Dependability
Being true to one's word even when it is difficult to carry out what was promised.

9. Diligence
Seeing every task as an assignment from the Lord and applying energy and concentration to accomplish it.

10. Discernment / Sensitivity
Knowing what to look for in evaluating people problems and things. Saying the right words at the right time.

11. Endurance
Maintaining commitment to a goal during times of pressure. Recognising and then laying aside hindrances.

12. Faith
Developing an unshakeable confidence in God's Word and visualising God's will and acting upon it.

13. Forgiveness
Choosing not to hold an offence against another. Remembering how much God has forgiven us.

14. Generosity
Recognising that all possessions belong to God. Being a wise steward of time, money and possessions. Being a cheerful giver.

15. Gentleness
Responding to needs in kindness and love. Knowing what is appropriate to meet the emotional needs of others.

16. Gratefulness
Recognising the benefits which God and others have provided; looking for appropriate ways to express genuine appreciation.

17. Hospitality
Providing an atmosphere that contributes to the physical and spiritual health of those around us.

18. Humility
Recognising our total inability to accomplish anything for God except by His grace. Recognising our fundamental neediness.

19. Initiative
Taking steps to seek after God with our whole heart. Assuming responsibility for the physical and spiritual encouragement of those around us. Giving first.

20. Loyalty
Adopting as one's own the wishes and goals of those who are being served.

21. Meekness
Yielding rights and possessions to God. Earning the right to be heard rather than demanding a hearing.

22. Patience
Accepting difficult situations as from God without giving Him or others a deadline to remove the problem.

23. Punctuality
Showing esteem for other people and their time by not keeping them waiting.

24. Reverence
Demonstrating to God and others, respect for the authority and character of God.

25. Security
Building affections and expectations around the person of Christ and His eternal Word.

26. Self-control
Quickly identifying and obeying the initial prompting of the Holy Spirit. Bringing thoughts, words and actions under the control of the Holy Spirit.

27. Sincerity
Having motives that are transparent. Having a genuine concern to benefit the lives of others.

28. Truthfulness
Gaining approval of others without misrepresenting the facts. Facing the consequences of a mistake. Telling the whole truth.

29. Virtue
Building personal moral standards that will cause others to desire a more godly life.

30. Wisdom
Seeing life from God's perspective. Applying principles of life in daily situations.

Emotions ...... How do you feel?

Friends respond to emotion with emotion.

Sometimes we find that we have a limited vocabulary to describe emotions and feelings. These faces, each depicting a particular emotion, may be useful when we struggle to find words to describe a feeling.

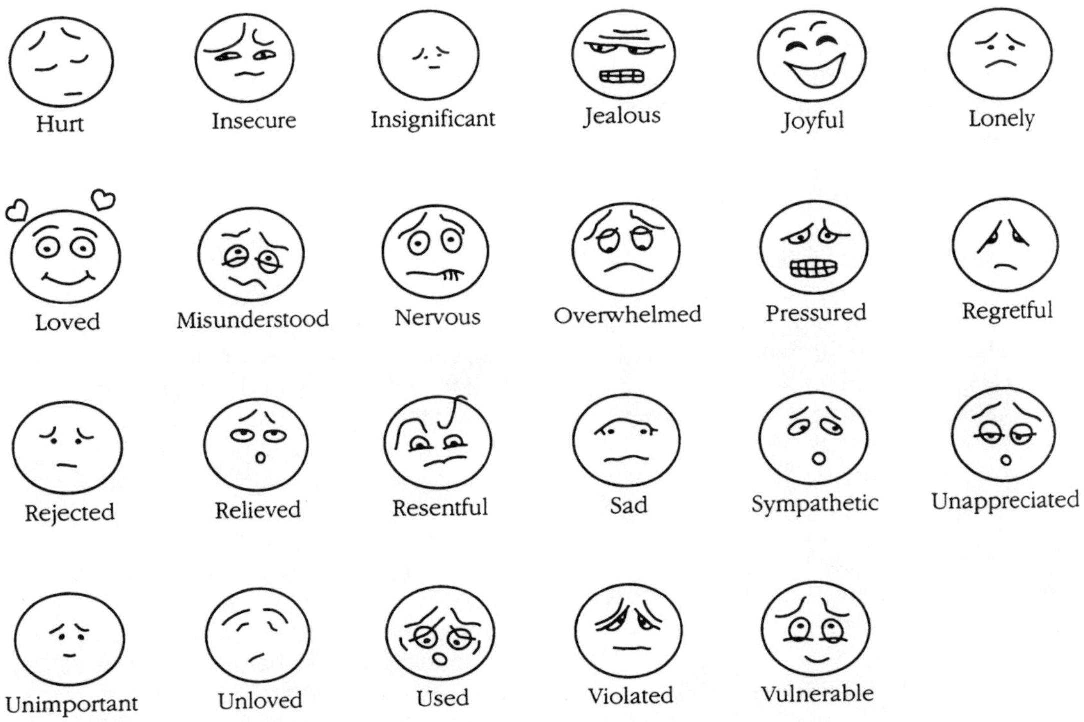
Hurt
Insecure
Insignificant
Jealous
Joyful
Lonely
Loved
Misunderstood
Nervous
Overwhelmed
Pressured
Regretful
Rejected
Relieved
Resentful
Sad
Sympathetic
Unappreciated
Unimportant
Unloved
Used
Violated
Vulnerable

Deepening Intimacy as Lovers

Lovers provide experiences of sharing and giving to each other - "Being together".

How do we view sexual intimacy?

Talking about sexual needs can often be difficult but being open with one another becomes more possible when we change how we talk about our sexual relationship.

If sex is viewed as something we "do" then it may easily be evaluated like other activities. e.g. How often? or What is the performance like?

If sex is viewed as something we "have" then it may become something we manage or conditionally agree to e.g. Once the decorating is finished; or: If you are home on time all week. Conflicts can follow over manipulations, bargaining or spouses who go on strike!

Sex is something that you share. Sexual intimacy is all about having the freedom to give all of yourself to your husband/wife. When we give to each other each partner feels cherished and valued.

It is sad that the sexual times a couple share can often lead to disappointment and be a "problem" between them. Sexual intimacy can be an area of frustration and a current painful issue for many couples. There may be anxiety and fear or anger and resentment associated with the sexual relationship. The target of deep mutual satisfaction sexually may feel an unobtainable goal.

Cultivating Romance

Anticipating a sexually intimate time together can increase romance, for instance parting in the morning with words expressing desire to be together at the end of the day.

Focus on giving not taking: "How might I increase your enjoyment?"

Give to each other emotionally first. Listen, share feelings, heal hurts, praise character qualities, enter the other's world.

Increase non-sexual touching.

The exercise known as a love map provides opportunity to talk to each other about sexual times together. It is good to share together, to laugh with one another. It would not be unusual for a wife's love map to begin several days prior to the sexually intimate time. e.g. As a lead up to Saturday night, come home on time on Wednesday. Have a meal together on Thursday and talk together. Go out together on Friday evening. This should not be confused with manipulating or bargaining. The time spent together on the three evenings leading up to Saturday are giving to the wife's emotional needs, preparing her to be able to give freely to her husband.

As you fill in your love map remember that your partnership is unique and enjoy the freedom that thought gives.

Love Map

"and the two shall become one flesh" Genesis 2:24

Background

Four of the major hindrances to sexual intimacy are addressed in this exercise.

1. Lack of openness/communication - Sex is not an easy subject to discuss for most couples; little experience or role modelling plus learned avoidance of the topic leaves many couples in a cycle of little openness, resentments and frustrations.
2. Unhealthy pre-occupation with "getting" rather than "giving" - tragically many of us (especially men) grew up with a mindset that sex was something to be taken, earned or manipulated; the art of giving oneself to another person is therefore foreign to us and awkward.
3. Boredom - Lack of creativity/freshness - "Sameness" produces complacency and feelings of obligation and duty, while creativity communicates initiative, desire and anticipation.
4. Lack of Anticipation and Expectancy - ***"as a man(or woman) thinks so is he(or she)!"*** Proverbs 23:7 Your mind is your most important sexual resource; learning to mentally anticipate times of being together with your spouse builds excitement, creativity and desire.

Completing your love map.
Each spouse completes the chart below in answer to this question:-
"From my point of view, an ideal sexually intimate time with my spouse would include the following" :

1	7
2	8
3	9
4	10
5	11
6	12

Include personally meaningful items related to timing, location, clothing and romantic preparations. You might want to consider personal preferences related to initiative, foreplay, positions and "after-play".

Marriage Intimacy - the freedom to SHARE all of oneself with another person....Body, soul and spirit.

- Exchange your "love maps" - pick a private time and place.
- Discuss them as much as you are comfortable - (you'll grow more comfortable as you repeat the exercise).
- Clarify and answer questions as appropriate.
- "Free" your spouse to fulfil as much of your love map as he/she is now comfortable with ...don't insist, get pushy, or love conditionally!

Give to one another Plan ahead two times of intimacy to fulfil both Love Maps.

- Husband should first "Give" in fulfilling his wife's Love Map - with a subsequent time for the wife to "Give".
- Plan a time for this so you can both anticipate it.
- Throughout the day, spend moments anticipating the pleasures of you "becoming one".
- Freely share all of yourself with one another.

Reflect, Experiment, Repeat the exercise.

Scatter and Share

After sharing with each other appreciation for character qualities exchange love maps.

Return to the group

As the last session is reached and the practice of the intimacy principles becomes established in your lives you may like to refer back to session one. Remind yourself of the assessment you gave of the level of intimacy you were experiencing in each of the three areas, physical, emotional and spiritual. Encourage one another as you share ways in which you feel your relationship has grown and deepened.

Share with each other 3 ways in which you would like to go on deepening your experience of intimacy

3 ways I would like to deepen our relationship

1. ______________________________

2. ______________________________

3. ______________________________

3 ways my husband/wife would like to deepen our relationship

1. ______________________________

2. ______________________________

3. ______________________________

Initmacy Action Plan		
What action is needed	**How will it happen**	**When will it happen**
1		
2		
3		
4		
5		

Prayer

Thank you for my marriage partner. Thank you for what we have shared and all you have taught us about how to enrich our marriage. Thank you Lord that you care about marriage relationships and that we know ours is special to you. We pray that our love for one another will continue to grow and be blessed by you.

Scatter and Share / Marriage Staff Meeting:

1. Talk about any calendar coordination, planning, goal evaluation, or expressions of appreciation that you need to do,

2. Complete this sentence:
"Three important things I especially want to remember and practice from this session are
a.

b.

c.

Share what you just wrote with your spouse. Then ask your spouse: "What would be three things you would especially like for me to remember and practice from this session?" Then write these three here:

a.

b.

c.

3. Continue to work on your "Intimacy Action Plan" as needed until you have agreed together as a couple on five "what to do" ideas, and you have agreed on a "how to" and "when" plan.

4. To share fully all that has been covered in this last session will take several staff meetings and there will also be issues from earlier sessions that you may wish to develop a lot further. Use the time today to put staff meetings into the diary. If you have been meeting for this course one evening a week you may find it possible to continue to preserve this same evening each week for your marriage. Remember that the times for fun you share are also important.

5. You may find it helpful to jot down the initial items you want to begin to devote time and to plan when you might do so.

6. Select one of these to begin working on in this meeting.

Close your time with "Perfect Love Praying." Ask God to enable you to especially remember and practice these three things your spouse has just vulnerably requested of you.

About the Authors

Dr. David and Teresa Ferguson are the directors of Intimate Life Ministries, which serves thousands of churches and ministry leaders worldwide with a message of how to deepen intimacy with God and deepen relationships in marriage, family and the church. Early in his church ministry David, like so many others in Christian ministry, tried unsuccessfully to achieve balance between ministry and family demands. Out of an intense desire to honor God and minister to the needs of his family, he rediscovered a **1st century Biblical principle** that transformed his life, his family and his ministry to others. For the past 20 years, he and his wife, Teresa, have been sharing that message in print, through ministry retreats, the media and in speaking engagements around the world.

David's graduate work in theology, counseling, and the social sciences focused on the Great Commandment Principle and its impact on relationships, ministry, and culture. David has a masters of education from Southwest Texas State University and doctor of philosophy an doctor of letters degrees from Oxford Graduate School. His is a member of the Oxford Society of Scholars.

David and Teresa have been married thirty-five years and have co-authored several previous books and numerous articles. They reside in Austin, TX, and have three adult children – Terri, Robin, Eric and a new grandchild – Zachary.

About Intimate Life Ministries

Who and What Is Intimate Life Ministries?
Intimate Life Ministries (ILM) is a training and resource ministry, headquarted in Austin, TX and Leamington Spa, England; whose purpose *is to assist in the development of Great Commandment ministries worldwide*, ongoing ministries that deepen our intimacy with God and with others in marriage, family, and the church. Intimate Life Ministries comprises:

- A network of **churches** seeking to fortify homes and communities with his love;
- A network of **pastors and other ministry leaders** walking intimately with God and their families and seeking to live vulnerably before their people;
- A team of **accredited trainers** committed to helping churches establish ongoing Great Commandment ministries;
- A team of **professional associates** from ministry and other professional Christian background, assisting with research, training, and resource development;
- **Christian broadcasters**, publisher, media, and other affiliates, cooperating to see marriages and families reclaimed as divine relationships;
- **Headquarters staff** providing strategic planning, coordination, and support.

Intimate Life Ministries

USA Office:
PO Box 201808
Austin, TX 78720
tel: (512) 795-0498
fax: (512) 795-0853
UK free phone 0800-966685

UK Office:
2 St. Mark's Road
Leamington Spa
Warwickshire
CV32 6DL
tel: (01926) 421004
fax: (01926) 435704